U.S. RESERVE FORCES

With the compliments of

Kermit Gordon

President

THE BROOKINGS INSTITUTION

1775 Massachusetts Avenue, N.W., Washington, D.C. 20036

Studies in Defense Policy
TITLES PUBLISHED

Naval Force Levels and Modernization:
An Analysis of Shipbuilding Requirements
Arnold M. Kuzmack

Support Costs in the Defense Budget: The Submerged One-Third
Martin Binkin

The Changing Soviet Navy
Barry M. Blechman

Strategic Forces: Issues for the Mid-Seventies
Alton H. Quanbeck and Barry M. Blechman

U.S. Reserve Forces: The Problem of the Weekend Warrior
Martin Binkin

MARTIN BINKIN

U.S. RESERVE FORCES
The Problem of the Weekend Warrior

A Staff Paper

THE BROOKINGS INSTITUTION
Washington, D.C.

Library of Congress Cataloging in Publication Data:
Binkin, Martin, 1928–
    U.S. reserve forces

    (Studies in defense policy)
    Includes bibliographical references.
    1. United States–Armed Forces–Reserves. I. Title.
II. Series.
UA42.B5   355.3'7'0973   73-23109
ISBN 0-8157-0959-5

9 8 7 6 5 4 3 2 1

THE BROOKINGS INSTITUTION is an independent organization devoted to nonpartisan research, education, and publication in economics, government, foreign policy, and the social sciences generally. Its principal purposes are to aid in the development of sound public policies and to promote public understanding of issues of national importance.

The Institution was founded on December 8, 1927, to merge the activities of the Institute for Government Research, founded in 1916, the Institute of Economics, founded in 1922, and the Robert Brookings Graduate School of Economics and Government, founded in 1924.

The Board of Trustees is responsible for the general administration of the Institution, while the immediate direction of the policies, program, and staff is vested in the President, assisted by an advisory committee of the officers and staff. The by-laws of the Institution state, "It is the function of the Trustees to make possible the conduct of scientific research, and publication, under the most favorable conditions, and to safeguard the independence of the research staff in the pursuit of their studies and in the publication of the results of such studies. It is not a part of their function to determine, control, or influence the conduct of particular investigations or the conclusions reached."

The President bears final responsibility for the decision to publish a manuscript as a Brookings book or staff paper. In reaching his judgment on the competence, accuracy, and objectivity of each study, the President is advised by the director of the appropriate research program and weighs the views of a panel of expert outside readers who report to him in confidence on the quality of the work. Publication of a work signifies that it is deemed to be a competent treatment worthy of public consideration; such publication does not imply endorsement of conclusions or recommendations contained in the study.

The Institution maintains its position of neutrality on issues of public policy in order to safeguard the intellectual freedom of the staff. Hence interpretations or conclusions in Brookings publications should be understood to be solely those of the author or authors and should not be attributed to the Institution, to its trustees, officers, or other staff members, or to the organizations that support its research.

FOREWORD

Although the debate over the level of U.S. military spending has brought a number of defense issues under public scrutiny, one set of issues—those bearing on military reserve forces—has escaped critical examination. Despite marked changes over the past decade in U.S. foreign policy, defense strategy, and active military force levels, the size, structure, and missions of the reserves have remained nearly constant. But the recent dramatic increase in the cost of military manpower suggests that an evaluation of the reserve forces is overdue. The end of the draft, which has given the reserves a more prominent role in national defense, makes such an assessment all the more important. This paper—the fifth in the Brookings series of Studies in Defense Policy—is an initial step in that assessment.

The author does not seek to prescribe the best mix of active and reserve forces, a task that would require a thorough reexamination of U.S. defense missions and strategic concepts. Rather, he focuses on efficiency, suggesting how the reserves could serve their present purposes at less cost in money and manpower. After examining the existing system, the military, political, and bureaucratic influences that have shaped it, and the mounting pressures for a break with the past, the author asks whether the reserves are assigned missions that have lost their relevance or that might be performed in less costly ways. He examines economies that could be achieved by substituting reserve for active personnel, thus taking advantage of the lower peacetime costs of reservists. And he asks whether, in the absence of the draft, enough volunteers can be attracted to the reserves without proposed additional financial incentives, and whether the reserve retirement system is more generous than necessary.

Taken together, the author's proposals call for substantial changes in the way the reserves function and in their relation to the active forces. To help overcome the political and institutional obstacles to such changes, he recommends that both the Congress and the staff of the National Security Council take a more active part in evaluating reserve force issues.

Martin Binkin, a senior fellow in the Brookings Foreign Policy Studies program, was formerly with the Office of the Assistant Secretary of Defense (Systems Analysis). He is the author of a previous Brookings staff paper, *Support Costs in the Defense Budget: The Submerged One-Third,* and co-author of *All-Volunteer Armed Forces: Progress, Problems, and Prospects,* a study published by the Senate Armed Services Committee.

The Institution is indebted to George H. Quester, Stanley R. Resor, General Matthew B. Ridgway, and Henry S. Rowen—members of its Defense Advisory Board—for their helpful comments on the manuscript. Others who gave generously of their time to comment include John F. Ahearne, Theodore C. Marrs, Gorman C. Smith, Colonel Ellis C. Stewart, and R. James Woolsey. Mr. Binkin thanks Commander Ted Baker, Barry M. Blechman, Colonel Delbert M. Fowler, Edward R. Fried, Colonel Richard D. Lawrence, Henry Owen, Alton H. Quanbeck, and others at Brookings for their comments and suggestions. He is also grateful to Louisa Thoron, who checked data sources and references; to Mary Miraglia, who typed the manuscript; and to Virginia C. Haaga for editing it.

The Institution acknowledges the assistance of the Ford Foundation, whose grant helps to support its work in defense studies. The views expressed herein are those of the author and should not be ascribed to the persons who commented on the manuscript, to the Ford Foundation, or to the trustees, officers, or other staff members of the Brookings Institution.

KERMIT GORDON
President

January 1974
Washington, D.C.

CONTENTS

Tables

Figure

CHAPTER ONE

INTRODUCTION

A key element of current U.S. national security strategy is the concept of "total force planning": using *all* appropriate resources—both U.S. and Free World—to capitalize on the potential of available assets. For U.S. military forces, this means concurrent consideration of total forces, active and reserve, to determine the most advantageous mix to support national strategy. As explained by one of the principal architects of the strategy, "Lower sustaining costs of non-active duty forces, as compared to the cost of maintaining larger active duty forces . . . allows more force units to be provided for the same cost as an all-active force structure, or the same number of force units to be maintained for lesser cost."[1]

What is an "appropriate" mix of active and reserve forces?[2] Views vary widely. On the one hand, some critics argue that recent experience with reserves, particularly their failure to be used in Vietnam—the longest and perhaps most difficult war in U.S. history—casts strong doubt on their value and raises serious questions about their future role in national security. On the other hand, with the end of the draft, the reserves have become the primary option available to the President for quickly expanding military forces in a national emergency.

An appropriate balance of active and reserve forces should rest principally on a technical assessment of military "requirements"—that is, the forces seen as necessary to meet the objectives of national security strategy. The overwhelming problems associated with sizing military forces are well recognized; not well recognized are the problems to be faced in deciding on a suitable active-reserve mix of those forces. The imprecise links among foreign policy,

1. *Statement of Secretary of Defense Melvin R. Laird on the FY 1972-1976 Defense Program and the 1972 Defense Budget, March 9, 1971*, p. 36.
2. The terms "reserves" and "reserve forces" are used interchangeably throughout this paper; in both cases national guard and reserve components are included.

defense strategy, and military force levels are made even more obscure in the case of reserve forces by the uncertainties as to when and how they might be used, how effectively they could be expected to perform, and how much weight they should be assigned in the deterrence formula. In short, an assessment of the best mix of reserve and active forces requires a thorough reexamination of the U.S. defense missions and strategic concepts, which is beyond the scope of this paper.

Nonetheless, important questions of efficiency remain that can be examined within the context of existing missions and strategic concepts. That is the object of this paper. It is the more important since the administration views reserve forces as a vital element in the U.S. military posture and calls for improvements in their capabilities and increases in their responsibilities.

The following statement by Secretary of Defense Melvin R. Laird in August 1970, which was designed to turn around the prevailing apathy toward the reserves and establish their credibility as a full partner in the defense mix, underlines this point: "Members of the National Guard and Reserve, instead of draftees, will be the initial and primary source for augmentation of the active forces in any future emergency requiring a rapid and substantial expansion of the active forces."[3] With this, the administration set about improving the readiness of the reserves, while apparently standing pat on their size, structure, and missions.

As a result, direct spending on reserve forces has increased over the past four years—from $2.6 billion in fiscal year 1970 to a peak of $4.4 billion in fiscal 1974. Furthermore, the reserve budget is consuming an increasing share of defense spending, reaching a high of over 5 percent in fiscal 1974. Also problems are expected in attracting enough volunteers to fill reserve units in the absence of pressure from the draft; financial incentives, mainly in the form of bonus payments, are the administration's recommendation to Congress.

As hard choices await national security planners, who are faced with fitting maximum defense capabilities within more limited defense resources, the following are among the key issues that come to the fore: What constitutes the requirement for reserves? Do all of the missions now assigned to them need to be performed? Are there better ways to use the reserves? Can they substitute for the more expensive active forces? These are the principal questions addressed in this paper.

The next three chapters describe the reserve forces—how they are composed, what they are designed to do, and how much they cost. They discuss

3. Laird, *Statement on FY 1972-1976 Defense Program,* p. 36.

the military, political, and bureaucratic factors that influence the shape of the reserves and the mounting pressures calling for a closer scrutiny of reserve force issues.

The rest of the paper explains the bases for possible changes in reserve forces and suggests three types of actions that could be taken to make the reserves a better national security bargain: pruning less effective units and personnel; substituting some selected reserve units for more costly active forces; and achieving economies in the reserve compensation system. It concludes that such changes, which would reduce reserve manpower by over 300,000 and active manpower by about 60,000 and save more than $1.4 billion annually, could be made without redefining U.S. national security interests and without altering current U.S. military strategy.

CHAPTER TWO

THE RESERVES TODAY

As they are now structured, U.S. reserve forces consist of seven components: Army National Guard, Army Reserve, Naval Reserve, Marine Corps Reserve, Air National Guard, Air Force Reserve, and Coast Guard Reserve. This chapter outlines the main characteristics of each (except for the Coast Guard Reserve)[1] —what they are, how they are composed, and how much they cost— and briefly discusses the implications that can be drawn for their future from the present course of events.

Organization

Reservists, in addition to being associated with one of the seven components listed above, are also identified with one of three categories: Ready Reserve, Standby Reserve, and Retired Reserve.

The *Ready Reserve,* the largest, with about 2.3 million personnel, consists of reservists who can be called to active duty by the President without congressional approval. This prerogative is not without conditions, however. The Congress limits the number of ready reservists—currently they cannot exceed 2.9 million—and limits the number that can be called to active duty by the President, currently 1 million.

Within the ready reserves, there are two categories: the Selected Ready Reserve and the Individual Ready Reserve. The former, which was created by the Congress in the Reserve Forces Bill of Rights and Vitalization Act of 1967, is characterized by the following: (a) it is composed almost exclusively of organized reserve units, (b) all of its members drill periodically and are paid, (c) it is composed entirely of "volunteers," although a large fraction of these are draft-motivated, and (d) its strength is authorized annually by the

---

1. The Coast Guard Reserve, which consists of about 11,000 members, is under the administrative and financial control of the Department of Transportation. It would come under the operational control of the U.S. Navy in time of war or national emergency.

Congress. For fiscal 1973, its authorized average strength was 977,000; for fiscal 1974, the administration has requested 911,000.

The individual ready reservists, on the other hand, are not members of units and generally do not train or get paid. Rather, they make up a manpower pool of previously trained personnel, liable to individual call-up at the discretion of the President under the guidelines outlined above. For the most part, these reservists are nonvolunteers fulfilling their reserve obligations.[2] At last count, the individual ready reservists numbered 1.4 million out of a total of 2.3 million ready reservists.

Members of the *Standby Reserve,* like the Individual Ready Reserve, do not train, nor are they paid. Unlike the Individual Ready Reserve, however, they can be called to active duty only with congressional approval. For the most part, standby reservists are completing their reserve obligation after performing a combination of active duty and required service in a ready reserve component. Congress does not limit the number of standby reservists; as of December 1972 they numbered 490,000. Since this group has little impact on the defense budget, and the conditions of their availability are highly uncertain, they have received little attention in defense planning circles. The fact that their number will probably dwindle in an all-volunteer environment, as fewer people serve in the military services for longer periods of time, has not aroused perceptible concern.

The *Retired Reserves,* presently numbering close to 700,000, are those who have qualified for retirement through length of service or disability. Under limited conditions, they are subject to call-up; for practical purposes, however, they represent a low potential for mobilization.

By way of summary, Table 2-1 shows, for each of the categories, recent strengths by reserve component and applicable mobilization guidelines.

Force Structure

Although the numbers of reservists are important indicators, particularly to the Congress and to analysts interested in comparisons of manpower levels,

2. The Armed Forces Reserve Act of 1952 and the Military Selective Service Act of 1967, as amended, provide a complex patchwork of active and reserve options for fulfilling a six-year military service obligation. Among the available options are the following: (1) three years active duty, two years individual ready reserve, one year standby reserve; (2) two years active duty, two years selected reserve, two years standby reserve; or (3) six months active duty and the remainder in selected reserve. Contrary to widespread belief, the six-year obligation did not expire with induction authority; as matters now stand, male volunteers will continue to incur this obligation.

Table 2-1. Military Reserve Forces, Numbers and Availability, December 31, 1972

Category	Actual strength Dec. 31, 1972 (in thousands)	Availability
Ready Reserve	**2,309**	Not more than one million members of the Ready Reserve may be on active duty without their consent (other than for training). They may be ordered to active duty in time of national emergency declared by the President, or when otherwise authorized by law, for not more than 24 consecutive months.
Selected Reserve		
Army National Guard	390	
Army Reserve	234	
Naval Reserve	128	
Marine Corps Reserve	40	
Air National Guard	91	
Air Force Reserve	48	
Subtotal	931	
Individual Ready Reserve		
Army Reserve	911	
Naval Reserve	200	
Marine Corps Reserve	130	
Air Force Reserve	137	
Subtotal	1,378	
Standby Reserve	**490**	Members of the Standby Reserve may be ordered to active duty (other than for training) only in time of war, or national emergency declared by Congress, or when otherwise authorized by law, for the duration of the war or emergency and for six months thereafter.
Army Reserve	332	
Naval Reserve	53	
Marine Corps Reserve	56	
Air Force Reserve	49	
Retired Reserve	**671**	A member of the Retired Reserve may, if qualified, be ordered to active duty without his consent in time of war or national emergency declared by Congress, or when otherwise authorized by law. . . . A member on an inactive status list or in a retired status may not be ordered to active duty . . . unless the secretary concerned, with the approval of the secretary of defense . . . determines that there are not enough qualified reserves in an active status or in the inactive national guard in the required category who are readily available.
Army Reserve	336	
Naval Reserve	110	
Marine Corps Reserve	2	
Air Force Reserve	223	

Source: Department of Defense, Office of the Assistant Secretary of Defense, Manpower and Reserve Affairs, March 1973, unpublished data. Figures are rounded.

they can also be misleading. For example, proponents of reserve forces have publicized the fact that "in the Selected Reserve of fiscal year 1973, we shall be supporting approximately 29 percent of our total U.S. military force at a cost of only 4.9 percent of the total defense budget."[3] The proportion of total available manpower that is in the reserve forces, however, is of limited use as a measure of military capability. The portion of the weight carried by the reserves can be assessed more realistically in terms of "force structure" or the primary symbols of military force (Army divisions, Naval ships, and Air Force squadrons). The major elements of the reserve force structure, which are summarized in Table 2-2, are discussed below.

Table 2-2. Major Elements of the Reserve Force Structure, by Component, Fiscal Year 1973

Army Reserve	*Naval Reserve*	*Air Force Reserve*
3 infantry brigades	Surface	24 tactical airlift squadrons
11 support brigades	31 destroyers	18 associate airlift squadrons
13 training divisions	4 destroyer escorts	5 air rescue squadrons
24 support commands	18 minesweepers	4 special operations squadrons
108 army hospitals	18 construction battalions	3 tactical fighter squadrons
65 separate battalions	Air	
	2 attack carrier wings	
	2 antisubmarine air groups	
	12 patrol squadrons	
	4 fleet tactical support squadrons	
Army National Guard	*Marine Corps Reserve*	*Air National Guard*
8 divisions	1 division	18 interceptor squadrons
18 separate brigades	1 air wing	26 tactical fighter squadrons
155 separate battalions		27 other tactical squadrons
4 armored cavalry regiments		21 airlift squadrons

Source: Department of Defense, "Annual Report of the Secretary of Defense on Reserve Forces, Fiscal Year 1972" (1973; processed), pp. 8, 22, III-4, III-6, VI-1, X-3, D-3, D-5, D-6; *Fiscal Year 1973 Authorization for Military Procurement*, Hearings, p. 1662.

Structure of the Reserves

The capability represented by the *Army Reserve* components can be measured in terms of "division force equivalents," consisting of combat divisions and their associated support. Each Army division requires about 48,000 men to conduct sustained combat operations, divided into three parts of approximately equal size (16,000 each):

3. *Fiscal Year 1973 Authorization for Military Procurement, Research and Development, Construction Authorization for the Safeguard ABM, and Active Duty and Selected Reserve Strengths*, Hearings before the Senate Armed Services Committee, 92 Cong. 2 sess. (1972), Part 3, p. 1617.

• The combat division itself—the major organizational unit—consists of battalion-sized elements that fight (for example, infantry, armor), prepare the battlefield and help fighting units maneuver and communicate (for example, combat engineers, aviation battalions), and supply, feed, and administer combat personnel and maintain their equipment (for example, transportation and maintenance battalions).

• An initial support increment (ISI) composed of nondivisional units that provide support to a combat division in the early stages of combat. These units are deployed with the division and provide support during the first sixty days of combat. Included are maintenance, supply, and medical units, as well as aviation, artillery, and air defense units.

• A sustaining support increment (SSI) composed of nondivisional units— similar to ISI units—that will be needed in the war area later to establish lines of communication and to provide rear-area combat forces. These units would probably not be needed until sixty days or more after the division was deployed.

In these terms, the Army Reserve components consist of eight combat divisions, complete with their sixteen initial and sustaining support increments, and the equivalent of twelve increments that would support active divisions, as is shown in Table 2-3. Additionally, a large number of separate nondivisional units complete the structure.

The *Naval Reserve* is geared mainly to providing individuals—rather than units—to augment the active forces. Of 128,000 reservists in the Selected Reserves in fiscal 1973, about 20 percent were in ship or aircraft units that would be mobilized as units. On the aviation side, the reserve force is composed of 2 carrier attack wings, 2 carrier antisubmarine air groups, 12 patrol

Table 2-3. Deployment of Army Division Forces, Active and Reserve, Fiscal Year 1973

Forces	Europe	Korea	Hawaii	United States	Total
Combat divisions					
Active	4 1/3	1	1	6 2/3	13
Reserve	...	...	...	8	8
Initial support increments					
Active	4 1/3	1	1	3 2/3	10
Reserve	...	...	...	11	11
Sustaining support increments					
Active	2 1/3	...	...	1 2/3	4
Reserve	...	...	...	17	17

Sources: Combat divisions: Department of Defense, "Military Manpower Requirements Report for FY 1973" (February 1972; processed), p. 119. Support increments: author's estimates, based on data in ibid., p. 31.

squadrons, and 4 fleet tactical support squadrons. Surface units are more diversified. They include 35 destroyer-type ships, 18 minesweepers, and 101 riverine craft, each with integrated crews, who are about one-half active and one-half reserve personnel. The individual augmentees, on the other hand, maintain their skills through association with a variety of training units— among them intelligence, telecommunications censorship, ordnance, and systems analysis.

The *Marine Corps Reserve* consists simply of a fully structured Marine Amphibious Force that, for practical purposes, is identical to its three active counterparts. It includes one division, one air wing, and associated combat and service support units. In general, these reserve units are provided with equipment and training similar to that received by the active forces.

The *Air Force Reserve* is largely an airlift organization, composed partly of units that have their own aircraft and partly of "associate" squadrons, whose reserve crews fly aircraft assigned to regular Air Force units. Units of the *Air National Guard* are involved mainly in air defense and tactical missions, including close air support, interdiction, and airlift. Together these Air Force components consist of about 1,300 units, squadron-size or smaller.

Table 2-4, which summarizes the major reserve force elements and compares them with similar elements in the active forces, shows that a large proportion (about 67 percent) of total manpower in the selected reserve is associated with Army Reserve components, which constitute a significant portion (43 percent) of total Army manpower (combined active and selected reserve). The Air Force, on the other hand, relies less on reserve manpower but has assigned to the Air Force Reserve a substantial portion of its tactical air missions.

Force Deployment Comparisons

The time required to deploy forces is not, strictly speaking, a measure of military capability; nevertheless, it provides a rough basis for estimating the relative effectiveness of active and reserve units. Reserve units cannot deploy as rapidly as can active units for two reasons. First, administrative tasks associated with gathering a group of citizen-soldiers are formidable. Business, financial, and family affairs need to be set in order. Military records and immunizations must be updated. In some cases, high-priority reserve units take special care to ensure that such administrative steps are current; indeed some Air Force Reserve tactical units have met deployment standards surpassing those set for active units. And second, in addition to these administrative delays, some reserve units need postmobilization training before deployment.

Table 2-4. Comparison of Major Elements in the Active and Reserve Forces, Fiscal Year 1973

Description	Active	Selected reserve	Total, active and selected reserve	Reserve as percent of total
Army				
Manpower (in thousands)	825	624	1,449	43
Division increments	13	8	21	38
Support increments	14	27 2/3	41 2/3	66
Air defense batteries	21	27	48	56
Navy				
Manpower (in thousands)	574	128	702	18
Surface ships	586	58	644	9
Carrier attack squadrons	70	10	80	12
Antisubmarine warfare squadrons	48	25	73	34
Marine Corps				
Manpower (in thousands)	197	40	237	17
Divisions	3	1	4	25
Air wings	3	1	4	25
Air Force				
Manpower (in thousands)	692	139	831	17
Tactical fighter squadrons	70	29	99	29
Other tactical squadrons	22	31	53	58
Tactical airlift squadrons	17	21	38	55
Continental air defense squadrons	7	18	25	72

Sources: Active manpower: *The Budget of the United States Government, Fiscal Year 1974*, p. 79; reserve manpower: Table 2-1 above; forces: Office of the Assistant Secretary of Defense, May 1973, unpublished data; Table 2-2 above; and *Air Force*, Vol. 56 (May 1973), p. 151.

Generally, the smaller the unit to be deployed, the less the need for training, all other things being equal. For example, if a unit is to be deployed at the squadron or company level, further training would be unnecessary if these units had met peacetime readiness standards. On the other hand, current criteria for the deployment of an Army National Guard division—as a division—calls for postmobilization training at the battalion, brigade, and division levels; this training could take up to fourteen weeks. Table 2-5 compares the deployability of some representative force elements for reserve and active forces. These estimates should be viewed with caution since they are subject to such wide variation. In view of recent mobilization experiences, many analysts take a much more conservative approach to estimating reserve deployability. Similarly, reserve enthusiasts question the capability of active units to deploy as quickly as it is claimed they can. One of the key issues, of course, is: How ready does a unit need to be before it can be deployed? In a major war, would

Table 2-5. Deployment Capability of Selected Active and Reserve Force Elements

Number of days between mobilization and deployment

Force element	Active	Reserve
Army		
Combat divisions	0–90	100–180
Support increments	0–90	30–90
Navy		
Carrier air wing	0–30	30–90
Marine Corps		
Division air wing	0–15	60–75
Air Force		
Tactical air wing	0–30	3–45

Source: Author's estimates, derived from information presented in various congressional hearings.

U.S. decision-makers refrain from deploying divisions until they attained a "fully ready" status? The estimates shown here do not allow for such judgments; rather they are based on current design criteria.

Cost of Reserve Forces

The full cost of U.S. reserve forces is difficult to pin down. The defense programming and budgeting structure permits, only in part, the separate identification of reserve costs.[4] Some are not charged directly to the reserve components—reserve retirement costs, support costs associated with reserve components but borne by the active forces, and the "opportunity costs" of equipment inherited from the active forces.

The Fiscal 1974 Reserve Budget

Considering visible costs first, the fiscal year 1974 budget includes $4.4 billion for the reserves, representing a high-water mark in reserve spending and doubling the fiscal year 1968 budget for reserve forces. As Table 2-6 shows, about one-half of this increase can be attributed to pay increases and price inflation. In real terms, fiscal 1974 reserve spending is up $1 billion over 1968, while total baseline[5] defense spending is at about the same level. Even viewed in this way, reserve spending trends constitute a real, though less

4. In the defense programming structure, the easily identifiable costs associated with reserve forces are aggregated in Program V—Guard and Reserve Forces.

5. Excluding the incremental costs associated with Vietnam.

Table 2-6. Reserve Forces Budget Trends, Selected Fiscal Years, 1964-74
Total obligational authority in billions of dollars

Description	1964	1968	1972	1973	1974
In current dollars					
Reserve budget	1.8	2.2	3.3	4.0	4.4
Total defense budget	50.7	75.6	77.7	80.9	85.0
Baseline defense budget[a]	50.7	56.4	70.7	74.7	82.1
Reserve budget					
as percentage of total budget	3.5	2.9	4.3	4.9	5.2
as percentage of baseline budget	3.5	3.9	4.7	5.4	5.4
In constant 1974 dollars					
Reserve budget	3.3	3.4	3.8	4.2	4.4
Total defense budget	84.5	108.9	86.8	85.1	85.0
Baseline defense budget[a]	84.5	82.4	79.1	78.7	82.1
Reserve budget					
as percentage of total budget	3.9	3.1	4.4	4.9	5.2
as percentage of baseline budget	3.9	4.1	4.8	5.3	5.4

Source: Basic data provided by the Office of the Assistant Secretary of Defense (Comptroller). Constant dollar costs for baseline and total differ from those used by the Department of Defense in one respect in that retired pay is calculated by multiplying the number of retirees each year by the average cost of retiree benefits in fiscal year 1974, rather than by applying fiscal year 1974 retirement costs to all previous years.

a. The baseline defense budget is that associated with peacetime forces. It excludes the incremental costs of the Vietnam war.

dramatic, reallocation of priorities. Table 2-7 shows the fiscal year 1974 reserve budget by component and appropriation category.

Among the nonvisible cost components, the value of equipment inherited from the active forces is the most significant. Equipment valued at over $850 million was issued in fiscal 1973 to Army Reserve components alone. This continued a program that was started in fiscal 1970 as U.S. forces began withdrawing from Vietnam. In that year $300 million worth of equipment was issued to Army Reserve units, followed by $725 million in fiscal 1971 and about $1 billion in fiscal 1972.[6] The Navy and Air Force do not separately identify the value of equipment transferred to their reserve components; how-

6. During the Vietnam war period, equipment issues to Army Reserve units virtually ceased. Equipment that had been ordered for the reserves in the early 1960s as a part of Secretary Robert S. McNamara's modernization programs was diverted to new active Army units as the military buildup started. By fiscal 1969, Army Reserve components had only one-third of the minimum equipment considered necessary for training. These shortages, along with a lack of training facilities, made it difficult to provide realistic training for reserve personnel. In retrospect, however, it would have been wasteful to procure *additional* equipment for the active forces during the buildup; if the Department of Defense had done so, it would today be accused of having equipment excesses—a charge that was common after earlier wars.

Table 2-7. Budget for Reserve Forces, by Component and Appropriation Category, Fiscal Year 1974

Total obligational authority in millions of dollars

Component	Military personnel	Operations and maintenance	Military construction	Procurement[a]	Total
Army National Guard	643.4	545.6	35.2	295.9	1,520.1
Army Reserve	522.2	264.1	40.7	78.1	905.1
Naval Reserve	222.5	167.5	17.9	6.2	414.1
Marine Corps Reserve	70.9	11.4	2.4	11.7	96.4
Air National Guard	191.2	525.7	20.0	30.5	767.4
Air Force Reserve	145.4	229.2	10.0	21.8	406.4
Subtotal	1,795.6	1,743.5	126.2	444.2	4,109.5
Active personnel support[b]	285.4	...	...	...	285.4
Total	2,081.0	1,743.5	126.2	444.2	4,394.9

Source: Department of Defense, Office of the Assistant Secretary of Defense, Manpower and Reserve Affairs, April 1973.

a. As is explained in the text, procurement costs shown do not include the value of equipment inherited from the active forces.

b. Cost of active personnel assigned to reserve activities, which are funded in active military personnel appropriations.

ever, according to one defense authority, "the statistics, if available, might be more impressive than those of the Army because of the unit value of major equipment items."[7] In recent years the Navy has replaced its obsolete World War II destroyers in the Naval Reserve, while Air Force Reserve components have modernized extensively with equipment inherited from the active forces as the Vietnam war has subsided.

The cost of this equipment is usually viewed as "sunk" and thus is not considered a part of the cost of reserve forces. It does however represent an "opportunity cost" since, if the active forces continued to use the equipment, their modernization might be postponed, though perhaps at some loss in military capability. Alternatively, the equipment could either be sold to foreign nations or provided to them under Military Assistance Programs. It is difficult to impute the costs with any precision. At the low extreme, the salvage value would be about $500 million; at most, the assigned cost could approach $3 billion. On the average, however, the opportunity cost probably falls in the lower half of this range.

Costs associated with activities of the regular forces that support reserve units are also difficult to estimate. For example, how much of the cost of

7. Theodore C. Marrs, "National Guard and Reserve Forces," prepared for the Air War College Associate Programs, printed in *Military Capabilities and Employment*, Vol. 3, 7th ed., Maxwell Air Force Base, Alabama: Air University, U.S. Air Force, March 1972, p. 8.

operating Andrews Air Force Base, which houses both active and reserve units, should be attributed to reserve forces? More measurable are the costs associated with training Air Force Reserve and National Guard pilots. In fiscal 1973, for example, about 430 were trained at a cost approaching $40 million, most of which was reflected in the active Air Force budget. On the other side of the question, costs absorbed by reserve forces in support of active units (for example, reserve units maintaining active equipment) deserve equal attention. Recent revisions in accounting practices within the Department of Defense should lead the way toward improvements in defining and allocating these support costs.

Finally, the costs of the reserve retirement system, which are included in total military retirement costs, do not appear in the reserve budget. In fiscal 1973, reserve retiree disbursements amounted to about $180 million, or 4 percent of the total $4.3 billion military retirement system budget.

Considering all the factors discussed above, the full annual costs for reserves are between $5 billion and $7 billion, depending mainly on how much of the value of inherited equipment is included in these costs.

Active-Reserve Cost Comparisons

The peacetime cost of operating a reserve unit is less than that for a similar active unit because (1) reserve military personnel are part time, thus commanding less pay than their full-time counterparts; (2) activity rates (training days, steaming hours, and aircraft flying hours) for a reserve unit are somewhat less than for a similar active unit, and thus smaller operations and maintenance costs are incurred; and (3) under existing policies, reserve personnel are not provided the same services as are full-time personnel (for example, recreational, travel, medical). Thus the support costs normally associated with active units are not as large for reserve forces.[8]

Differences in pay between active and reserve personnel can be seen in Table 2-8, which shows that on average full-time military receive pay and allowances approximately five times larger than that of reservists. This differential derives principally from the fact that the average reservist drills one weekend a month (considered the equivalent of four days for pay purposes) and normally participates in a two-week summer training program, a total of

---

8. Peacetime costs are, of course, the relevant ones for comparing active and reserve forces since, once the reserves are mobilized, there should be no significant differences. Also this discussion is limited to operating costs (military personnel, and operations and maintenance appropriations) since investment costs, if mobilized capabilities are to be equivalent, would be approximately the same whether a unit were active or reserve.

Table 2-8. Average Annual Per Capita Personnel Costs by Service, Active and Reserve Forces, Fiscal Year 1974[a]

In 1974 dollars

Service	Active	Reserve[b]
Army	9,428	1,940
Navy	9,878	1,926
Marine Corps	8,477	1,851
Air Force	10,910	2,419
Total, Department of Defense	9,905	2,009

Source: Derived from data provided by the Department of Defense, Office of the Assistant Secretary of Defense, February 1973. Included in the amounts is the estimated effect of the October 1973 military pay increase.

a. Includes basic pay, allowances, clothing, subsistence, and permanent-change-of-station allowances.

b. Army and Air Force Reserve costs are a composite of their Reserve and National Guard components.

sixty days' pay a year. The differences among the services stem from different distributions with respect to grade and years of service for pay purposes.

Differences in activity rates also give rise to lower reserve costs, but to a lesser extent. Equipment and weapon systems in the possession of reserve units are operated more intensively, and, for some units, utilization rates closely approach those of their active counterparts. For example, fighter aircraft assigned to active Air Force squadrons that are flown about 350 hours a year would be flown perhaps 300 hours a year if they were assigned to Air National Guard units. The cost differential is narrowed further since guard units rely more heavily on full-time civilian technicians,[9] whose costs appear in the operations and maintenance—rather than the military personnel—appropriations category. At the extreme, for those reserve units having a peacetime operational mission (for example, Army missile defense and Air Force interceptor units), the operating costs could approximate those of active units performing the same mission.

Active forces also have a much larger overhead cost component. Included are the costs associated with training and reassignment owing to more rapid personnel turnover and those accompanying the wide variety of services (education, medical, recreation) provided to active personnel.

9. Civilian technicians are a full-time cadre that prepare and execute operational and training programs and maintain equipment. In most cases, these technicians also hold military positions in the reserve unit. Thus, when a unit is mobilized, these civilians take on their military rank, which in some cases is at the general officer level. In fiscal 1973, about 73,000 civilians were assigned to reserve components, of which 51,000 were in Army and Air Force National Guard units.

Table 2-9, which combines the direct and indirect components discussed above, shows for each service the average annual peacetime operating cost for some major force elements common to both active and reserve forces. Also shown, for comparison, are the deployability estimates discussed earlier. The nature of the trade-off between active and reserve units is seen to vary among the components. The more substitutable units (Air Force and Navy) show the smallest cost differentials. This is not coincidental; a higher proportion of their costs is related to the operations and maintenance of equipment (where the differences are small) rather than to military personnel (where the differences are large). By implication, Air Force Reserve components could take responsibility for a greater share of the Air Force mission without substantially compromising deployment capability, but also without substantially reducing costs. On the other hand, larger savings would accrue from having more land combat units in the reserves, though this would mean a greater sacrifice in deployment capability.

Implications for the Future

Programs to improve the readiness of reserve forces as reflected in recent budgets, if they are continued, are certain to result in future growth in reserve spending. Defense Department officials have said that fiscal 1973 equipment issues "put us well on the way to attaining our equipment objectives for early deployment units . . . and will have produced visible progress in equipping the remaining units of these components. According to our present program, all the units of the Army's Reserve components should be at or near authorized equipment levels within the next four years."[10] The total value of equipment considered necessary for the mobilization of Army Reserve components is estimated at about $6 billion. With equipment at the end of fiscal 1973 valued at about $4 billion, and allowing for depreciation and retirement, the schedule conveyed above implies that about $1 billion worth of equipment will be issued annually over the next four years.[11]

10. *Fiscal 1973 Authorization for Military Procurement,* Hearings, Part 3, p. 1623.

11. This assumes that 10 percent of the equipment on hand needs to be repaired, replaced, or modified each year, based on an average life of about ten years for military equipment. Whether or not these costs will represent real increases is unclear. Much depends on the answer to the following question: When components have been fully equipped, will the total force (active and reserve) receive each new inventory item, or will the practice of "hand-me-downs" be resumed? The former option has potentially large financial impacts; the latter would signify a return to the earlier practice of viewing reserves as beneficiaries of "cast-off" equipment from active forces, perhaps in part to justify the cost-effectiveness of new generations of military hardware for the active forces.

Table 2-9. Comparison of Average Annual Peacetime Operating Costs and
Deployability for Selected Active and Reserve Force Elements, by Service

Force elements	Active forces		Reserve forces	
	Cost (in millions of dollars)	Deployability[a]	Cost (in millions of dollars)	Deployability[a]
Army				
Combat divisions	290	0–90	45	100–180
Support increments	290	0–90	45	30–90
Navy				
Carrier air wing	80	0–30	38	30–90
Marine Corps				
Division/Wing	480	0–15	82	60–75
Air Force				
Tactical air wing	45	0–30	23	3–45

Sources: Army active division costs: *Fiscal 1973 Authorization for Military Procurement,* Hearings, Part 1, p. 52; figures include a 16,500-man division increment with associated training and logistic support. Navy active carrier air wing costs: *CVAN-70 Aircraft Carrier,* Joint Hearings before the Joint Armed Services Subcommittee of the Senate and House Armed Services Committees, 91 Cong. 2 sess. (1970), p. 109; figures are for Forrestal class air wing, inflated to fiscal 1973 dollars. Air Force costs: "Value and Cost of the Reserves II," *The Officer* (December 1971), p. 6. Figures are based on data for an F4E wing; costs for which sources are not listed above are author's estimates.
a. Number of days between mobilization and deployment.

Beyond the problems associated with equipping reserve units, attention has also been directed to the problem of training facilities. Army Reserve units are widely dispersed, and few are located with active units. Particularly affected are combat and combat support units in metropolitan areas. For such units, little realistic training can be done in weekend drills at armories or training centers, and finding suitable nearby land for carrying out maneuvers presents a formidable problem. At the beginning of fiscal 1973, about 60 percent of maneuver units were without weekend training areas.[12] The total cost of a ten-year program (started in fiscal 1970) to overcome these deficiencies—as well as to improve existing facilities—is estimated at $840 million.[13] Moreover, as facilities become available, additional resources will be consumed in training exercises. Included in the latter are expenses associated with transportation, supplies, petroleum, oil, lubricants, and contractor services. The additional operations and maintenance funds needed to attain desired levels of readiness could approach $100 million a year—an increase of 15 percent over current funding levels.

12. *Fiscal 1973 Authorization for Military Procurement,* Hearings, Part 3, p. 1684.
13. *Annual Defense Department Report, Fiscal Year 1974,* Statement of Secretary of Defense Elliot L. Richardson before the Senate Armed Services Committee on the FY 1974 Defense Budget and FY 1974-1978 Program, March 28, 1973, pp. 76-77.

As the administration moves to provide reserve units with better equipment and training facilities, a new problem is taking shape. Under pressure of the draft, reserve units have had little difficulty in maintaining adequate manning levels. However, with the end of conscription, it is anticipated that reserve units will have problems in attracting enough volunteers. It is too early to tell what financial incentives will be necessary to meet manning goals; a rough indication is provided by the $85 million included in the fiscal 1974 defense budget for reserve enlistment and reenlistment bonuses.

All of this suggests that increases in the level of reserve spending will be needed merely to attain desired readiness for existing reserve forces. The many uncertainties make it difficult to estimate financial implications with any precision; however, a 25 percent real increase in reserve spending over the next several years to maintain the present course would not be extraordinary. The actual increase, in current dollars, would be even greater, of course, because of inflation.

CHAPTER THREE

THE RATIONALE FOR RESERVES

The basic rationale for maintaining reserve forces rests on economic grounds. If resources were unlimited, enough active forces could be maintained to meet all possible contingencies. Or if forward deployments or early deployments were considered unnecessary, all forces could be reserves. Since neither is the case, some mix of those forces provides maximum military capability within a given budget level or, alternatively, provides a given level of capability at a minimum cost. General economic theory provides conceptual allocation models for finding the "best" mix of active and reserve forces. In practice, however, they are difficult to use because of the problems associated with defining the relative costs and capabilities of active and reserve units.

These difficulties have in part served to discourage analysts and decision-makers from coming to grips with the force-mix issue and have permitted a host of nonmilitary factors to exert a strong influence in shaping the reserve structure. And, while requirements for active military forces are becoming better understood, a detailed rationale for reserve forces has remained outside the range of debate. This problem is in large part related to the way in which top decision-makers have envisaged the overall role reserves play in maintaining national security; their views have varied widely over the past three decades.

Use of Reserves: World War II to Vietnam

Between World War II and the Korean war the reserves were looked upon mainly as an expansion base for total and prolonged mobilization. They provided a pool of trained men that could be used as cadres to help train, organize, and equip the large number of citizen soldiers that would be called upon in a massive mobilization. This planning was consistent with the only type of contingency then contemplated—a replay of World War II.

The Korean war, however, introduced new concepts into national security planning; the terms "limited war" and "partial mobilization" were added to the defense vocabulary. The United States, finding itself with a total armed force of about 1.5 million men in 1950, faced the need for a rapid buildup of manpower. Although they were far from completely mobilized, reservists accounted for 35 percent of the buildup that occurred in the first year of that war.

As the United States adopted the strategy of massive retaliation following the Korean experience, the full mobilization role of the reserves appeared even more out of date. Protracted conventional wars were viewed as highly unlikely, emphasis was put on deterrence through forces in being, and a rapid-response role for reserve forces began to take shape. The quick-response role was further crystallized as national strategy under President Kennedy turned from massive retaliation to flexible response. Secretary of Defense McNamara stated it succinctly in 1961:

In the light of the present world situation, it is essential that [the Army] reserve forces be brought as soon as possible to a state of readiness that would permit them to respond on very short notice to limited war situations which threaten to tax the capacity of the active Army. Moreover, they must be so organized, trained and equipped as to permit their rapid integration into the active Army.[1]

Although U.S. involvement in Vietnam would have appeared to fit this model perfectly, reserves were not used except for the token mobilizations connected with the Pueblo incident and the Tet offensive in 1968. The decision not to rely on reserve forces for Vietnam could be interpreted as coming full circle to the early post–World War II use of reserves as an expansion base for complete mobilization only. In part, the absence of clear-cut guidelines for the use of reserve forces stems also from their unique value in the foreign policy arena. The inordinately high "political costs" and dramatic consequences associated with mobilizing citizen-soldiers in a democratic society makes them particularly useful as an instrument for signifying resolve. The mobilizations at the time of the Berlin, Cuban, and Pueblo crises are examples; in none of the cases could the call-up have been justified solely on grounds of military necessity. That this can also work in the opposite direction was sug-

1. Statement by Secretary of Defense Robert S. McNamara in *Department of Defense Appropriations for Fiscal Year 1967,* Hearings before the Senate Subcommittee on Department of Defense of the Committee on Appropriations and the Committee on Armed Services, 89 Cong. 2 sess. (1966), Part 1, p. 100.

gested by the Vietnam buildup experience, when President Johnson's decision *not* to mobilize reserves was made partly to demonstrate his intent to limit U.S. involvement.

Domestic Role of Reserves

Also during the Vietnam era, the domestic role of reserve components became prominent. National Guard components—both Army and Air Force—have the mission of providing state governors with the military forces needed to cope with local disturbances and emergencies. Between January 1965 and October 1971, guard units were used to maintain order during civil disturbances on 260 occasions; in the twenty prior years they were used only 88 times for this purpose.[2] The maximum number called at one time was about 13,000—in connection with the riot in Watts, California, in 1965. Civil disturbances also spread to college campuses in the late 1960s. The Kent State violence in 1970 focused increased attention on the possible disadvantages of using military reserve units to quell disorders, with particular scrutiny aimed at training and leadership and the guidelines under which these units would operate when mobilized.[3]

Also, as part of an effort to improve their public image, a wider public service role for reserves can be seen emerging. Their entrance into social welfare, pollution and erosion control, and other domestic community-action programs has been evident. For example, during their 1973 summer encampment, one Air Force Reserve unit had scheduled several projects as part of its "commitment to serve the community," including sponsoring a Red Cross blood drive and providing manpower to repaint facilities for emotionally disturbed children.[4]

2. "Training and Equipping the Army National Guard for Maintaining Order During Civil Disturbances," Report to the Congress by the Comptroller General of the United States (U.S. General Accounting Office, Sept. 8, 1972; processed), p. 1.

3. In addition to mobilizing guard units, the President can provide active military forces for these purposes. Governors have requested active force support on four occasions since the end of World War II. The peak deployment of 23,000 active troops for this purpose occurred after the murder of Dr. Martin Luther King. See Herman Boland, "The Reserves," *Studies Prepared for the President's Commission on an All-Volunteer Armed Force,* Vol. 2 (1970), p. IV-2-44. Prior to 1969, the President was also authorized to use reserve as well as guard units for these purposes. The authorizing legislation, which expired in that year, has not been renewed. Thus, to commit these reserve units in a civil disturbance would require a "declaration of a national emergency" by the President. See Comptroller General of the United States, "Report to the Congress," pp. 3-4.

4. *Chicago Tribune,* June 22, 1973.

Looking to the Future

With the end of conscription in July 1973, the reserves—for the first time in over two decades—have replaced the draft as the principal means for expanding military forces in a national emergency. Indeed, as the law now stands, the President may, by his own authority, exceed the authorized military manpower ceiling *only* by mobilizing reserves.[5] Despite this apparent increase in their level of responsibility, and the accompanying increase in their funding at the expense of other elements of the defense program, their precise role in current national security planning remains unclear. One Department of Defense study summarized the situation as follows:

In the Army Guard and Reserve there are more than 4,000 units of varying size . . . organized into 172 maneuver battalions and of these 15 have specific unit missions that are attached to force units; 15 more have a European mission and are attached to Active units; the remaining 142 have "general theater orientation" missions—meaning they are programmed to be sent to some region in the world but have no specific mission beyond that. The Air Guard, on the other hand, has the most specific statement of mission of all Reserves. Its units (including support) appear in three contingencies simultaneously. The Navy and Marine Corps Reserves have a general mission to be prepared to fight any contingency that may occur but have no specific unit missions.[6]

That they appear to be suited principally to a conventional war of indefinite duration, however, can be deduced by examining the capabilities of the

5. This provision, informally known as the "Kennedy-Stennis" amendment (after its principal sponsors, Senators Edward F. Kennedy and John C. Stennis), specifies that the authorized military end strengths "shall not include members of the Ready Reserve of such armed force ordered to active duty. . . ." The intent "is to require the use of the training Reserves to meet additional manpower requirements prior to the induction of additional personnel beyond the strengths authorized." (See *Authorizing Appropriations for Fiscal Year 1973 for Military Procurement, Research and Development, and for Anti-Ballistic Missile Construction; and Prescribing Active Duty and Reserve Strengths,* H. Rept. 92-1388, 92 Cong. 2 sess. (1972), pp. 3 and 21.) There is another—but less well known—option available to the President to raise military manpower without needing to seek congressional approval so long as authorized ceilings are not exceeded. Although normal induction authority contained in the Military Selective Service Act lapsed on July 1, 1973, authority to induct persons who have previously been deferred continues. Such individuals are subject to induction until age thirty-five. For practical purposes, however, most observers agree that this pool of manpower—numbering over one million—would not be called upon except in case of full mobilization. See description of the termination clause, Section 17 of the Military Selective Service Act in *Military Selective Service Act with Analysis,* House Armed Services Committee Report 92-41, 92 Cong. 2 sess. (1972), p. 8027.

6. "Economic Resource Analysis of Reserve Components" (Office of the Assistant Secretary of Defense [Manpower and Reserve Affairs—Systems Analysis], October 1971; processed), p. 25.

principal reserve elements discussed above. For example, by current standards, Army National Guard combat units are designed to attain readiness at the company level; postmobilization training to attain battalion, brigade, and division readiness would delay division-size deployments for perhaps four months. A large portion of the remaining Army Reserve forces—the sustaining support increments—are designed to reinforce the combat divisions only after sixty days of combat. Air Force Reserve units include a large proportion of long-range, multipurpose aircraft designed primarily for long-range interdiction, and Naval Reserve forces are structured to sustain a logistic pipeline to Europe or project air power ashore—both appropriate to longer wars. Apart from these major reserve forces, many of the smaller reserve support activities also appear to be designed solely for a World War II-type conflict. The latter include civil affairs units, whose members train to administer the daily civilian affairs of countries that the United States might occupy; other units are concerned with censorship and postal service.

On the other hand, the early deployment and multimission capabilities of some Air Force Reserve units make them particularly adaptable to a broad range of emergency uses. A small number of select Army Reserve units with early deployment capabilities could probably also be used to advantage in an emergency that called for a quick response. Such forces, however, comprise only a small part of total reserve forces and a small part of the reserve budget.

CHAPTER FOUR

PRESSURES FOR AND AGAINST CHANGE

The relation between U.S. reserve forces and national security strategy, explored in the previous chapter, strongly suggests that the size and shape of the reserve establishment is affected by factors other than military requirements. This chapter examines the nonmilitary influences on the structure of the reserves and recent pressures that appear to change their relative importance, thus calling for an assessment of reserve forces on the basis of military necessity alone.

Pressures to Maintain the Status Quo

The size and structure of the current reserve forces have been shaped largely by two nonmilitary factors. The influence of domestic politics on reserve forces has been widely publicized. Less obvious, but just as important, have been the institutional rivalries between the active and reserve components in each military service. These counterbalancing factors have tended to perpetuate the status quo.

The influence of domestic politics on reserve forces is markedly different from that bearing on active forces. The threat to close an active military installation, inactivate a military unit, or cancel the development or production of a weapon system meets with political opposition principally because of the economic impact it would have on the community concerned. Such action, it is feared, reduces employment opportunity and decreases community income, thus exacting high political costs.

Domestic Politics and the Reserves

In the case of reserves, however, it is necessary to look beyond these economic implications. Most reservists are otherwise employed full time and depend little on their reserve income; moreover, the size of reserve units is

24

Table 4-1. Representation on Selected Congressional Committees of
Members of Congress Who Are Reservists

Committee	Total number of members	Number who are reservists
Senate Armed Services	15	7
House Armed Services	43	12
Senate Appropriations	26	5
Defense Subcommittee	13	3
House Appropriations	55	13
Defense Subcommittee	12	5
Senate Veterans' Affairs	9	3
House Veterans' Affairs	26	9

Source: Compiled from data appearing in *Petition for a Writ of Certiorari to the United States Court of Appeals for the District of Columbia Circuit,* Elliot L. Richardson, Secretary of Defense, *et al.,* Petitioners *v.* Reservists Committee to Stop the War, *et al.,* Case No. 72-1188, U.S. Supreme Court, October Term 1972, App. D, pp. 49-51, and in *Congressional Directory,* 93 Cong. 1 sess. (1973).

such that any reduction would have a relatively small impact on the economic well-being of a community. What, then, makes the Congress sensitive to reductions in reserve forces? The answer rests primarily on broad grass-roots support and a strong well-organized lobby.

Reserve units, which can be found in about five thousand separate U.S. communities, are a part of the "intricate and subtle political chain that laces the country, running through village council rooms, county courthouses, and state capitals to Congress and the White House."[1] In many small towns, the armory is the hub of community social activities. Political pressure is brought to bear directly on members of Congress through local leaders (in the case of state guard units, through adjutant generals and governors) and indirectly through the Washington-based Reserve Officer and National Guard Associations—both of which are prosperous, united, articulate, and highly active organizations. A former member of the White House staff described the influence of the reserve lobby as follows:

Eco-political movements are nowhere more clearly visible than in the status of the National Guard and Reserve programs. . . . These citizen soldiers are so solidly entrenched politically that no one in Washington dares challenge them frontally.[2]

1. Martha Derthick, "Militia Lobby in the Missile Age—The Politics of the National Guard," in Samuel P. Huntington (ed.), *Changing Patterns of Military Politics* (Crowell-Collier, 1962), p. 192.
2. Douglass Cater, *Power in Washington: A Critical Look at Today's Struggle to Govern in the Nation's Capital* (Random House, 1964), p. 41.

The fact that 108 members of the 93d Congress (about one-fifth of the total) hold membership in one of the reserve components also has important political implications. As Table 4-1 shows, they are disproportionately represented on many of the major committees concerned with reserve legislation. The constitutionality of this dual status has been questioned, and the issue is currently in litigation.[3]

The influence of politics in the shaping of reserve forces has been vividly demonstrated. For three successive years starting in 1964, the administration tried unsuccessfully to merge Army Reserve and Guard components, reduce their combined strength by sixty thousand, and save about $150 million a year. After two years of stopgap legislation, the Congress effectively blocked such proposals by including in the Reserve Forces Bill of Rights and Vitalization Act of 1967 a provision that each component of the selected reserve must consist in part of organized units. Thus, by permanent law, some units have to be retained in separate Army Guard and Reserve components.

The 1967 legislation also included a requirement that the personnel strengths of the selected reserves be authorized on an annual basis before funds could be appropriated for their pay and allowances. This meant that reserve strengths would thereafter be set annually by the Armed Services Committees. According to Secretary of Defense Robert S. McNamara, the Army Reserve drill strengths so authorized by the Congress for fiscal 1968—the first year of authorization—were "more than we believe to be required to support our current contingency plans."[4]

3. A complaint filed in 1970 by a national association, the Reservists Committee to Stop the War, sought a judicial declaration that all members of the Congress who hold reserve commissions do so in violation of Article I, Section 6, Clause 2 of the U.S. Constitution, which provides that: "No Senator or Representative shall, during the Time for which he was elected, be appointed to any Civil Office under the Authority of the United States, which shall have been created, or the Emoluments whereof shall have been increased during such time; and no Person holding any Office under the United States, shall be a Member of either House during his Continuance in Office." The U.S. District Court, holding that membership in the reserves is an "office under the United States," ruled that members of Congress are "ineligible to hold a commission in the Armed Forces Reserve during [their] continuance in office." The Court of Appeals in October 1972 affirmed that opinion, and in April 1973 the Supreme Court agreed to review the case. See *Brief for the Petitioners,* James R. Schlesinger, Secretary of Defense, *et al.,* Petitioners *v.* Reservists Committee to Stop the War, *et al.,* Case 72-1188, U.S. Supreme Court, October Term 1973. For identification of members of the 93d Congress who are members of reserve components, see *Petition for a Writ of Certiorari to the United States Court of Appeals for the District of Columbia Circuit,* Elliot L. Richardson, Secretary of Defense, *et al.,* Petitioners *v.* Reservists Committee to Stop the War, *et al.,* Case No. 72-1188, U.S. Supreme Court, October Term 1972, App. D, pp. 49-51.

4. *Department of Defense Appropriations for 1968,* Hearings before Subcommittees of the House Committee on Appropriations, 90 Cong. 1 sess. (1967), Part 2, p. 335.

To protect the reserves from those who would threaten reductions in their size, the Congress authorizes each year *minimum* strength levels for reserve components. This is in contrast to other programs covered by annual defense authorization bills for which the amounts authorized are ceilings; for example, the Congress annually authorizes *maximum* active duty strengths. This preoccupation with minimum paid-drill strengths stems largely from the incentive structure in the current reserve compensation system, which is keyed to earning retirement benefits at age sixty. To earn these benefits a reservist must accumulate the necessary number of creditable "points" each year. These points can be earned in a variety of ways, but most lucratively through unit participation. Hence, the pressure exists to preserve paid-drill billets.[5]

More recently, budgetary considerations, along with anticipated problems in attracting enough volunteers (which are discussed below), caused the administration to request fiscal 1974 reserve strengths 66,000 below fiscal 1973 authorizations. This cut in reserve manpower, the first major one proposed during the Nixon administration, apparently raised strong opposition from reserve lobby groups. A subcommittee of the House Armed Services Committee reportedly offered to restore 4,500 billets in the Naval Reserve, which the Navy declined. Subsequently, however, these billets were restored by the Senate Armed Services Committee, with the difference being split in conference.[6]

What remains unclear, however, is whether the Congress would continue to fall under the influence of lobby groups and the strong advocates of the reserves among its membership if it were convinced that changes in the size, structure, and mission of the reserves could improve military capability without increasing defense spending, on the one hand, or decrease costs without compromising capability, on the other.

Bureaucratic Rivalries

In part, the congressional advocacy of reserve forces probably developed to counter the institutional biases in the Department of Defense against reserves. Mendel Rivers, the late chairman of the House Armed Services Committee, put the blame mainly on civilian leaders in the Pentagon. Referring to previous assurances that improvements in the readiness of reserve units would be made, he said,

5. The reserve retirement system is discussed further in Chapter 7 below.
6. See "Navy Reaffirms Drill-Strength Cut," *Navy Times*, June 20, 1973, p. 3, and *Authorizing Appropriations, Fiscal Year 1974, for Military Procurement, Research and Development, Active Duty and Reserve Strength, Military Training, Student Loads, and Other Purposes*, S. Rept. 93-467, 93 Cong. 1 sess. (1973), p. 40.

The Department of Defense and particularly its civilian executives have only given lipservice to these assurances. The lack of Reserve readiness is directly the result of the failure of the Pentagon to discharge its duties and responsibilities. Therefore, it is evident that Congress must exercise its constitutional authority "to raise armies" and stipulate in the statutory requirements that they will and must be met.[7]

Deep rivalries have traditionally existed between the active and reserve military factions in each service. The natural cleavage between professional and citizen soldiers widens in the face of a shrinking availability of defense resources. A sharpening of this competition was reflected by a key Pentagon official in testimony presented to the Senate Armed Services Committee, in which he identified as one of the major constraints to the development of a visible and credible reserve force "Ingrained attitudes—the 'we versus they' approach—the declination of responsibility for Guard/Reserve problems—the view that any move to upgrade reserves would downgrade Active Forces."[8]

These attitudes were particularly evident during the McNamara era, when the defense program was controlled principally through force levels (numbers of divisions, ships, and wings). Military planners had little incentive to suggest improvements in the reserve components for fear that reserve units would be viewed as closer substitutes for the regular forces.

The competition between active and reserve forces became more explicit under Secretary Melvin R. Laird's management approach. The "participatory management concept" provided the Joint Chiefs of Staff and military services with greater latitude in structuring forces within a fixed budget, including the specification of the active-reserve mix. Since the military services opposed the development of a greater reserve capability at the expense of the active forces, Laird found it necessary to earmark reserve funds and otherwise provide specific guidelines to ensure their priority in the programming and budgeting process.

On balance, these political and institutional factors discourage changes in the size and structure of the reserve forces. This is nowhere more evident than at the highest national policymaking levels. Over 150 studies have been directed by the National Security Council between 1969 and 1973, covering a wide variety of national security issues; none called for a comprehensive assessment of reserve forces. Moreover, the reserve budget appeared to have little trouble

7. *Congressional Record,* Vol. 113, Part 3, 90 Cong. 1 sess. (1967), p. 3836.

8. Statement by Dr. Theodore C. Marrs, Deputy Assistant Secretary of Defense for Reserve Affairs in *Fiscal Year 1973 Authorization for Military Procurement,* Senate Hearings, Part 3, p. 1625.

surviving annual reviews by the efficiency-minded Office of Management and Budget.

As a result, the size of reserve forces has been relatively insensitive to rather broad changes in U.S. foreign policy and defense strategy that would have appeared to call for a reform of the reserves on the basis of technical assessment alone. To national leaders, however, the financial cost of the status quo probably appeared small. Until recently, there was relatively little pressure to reduce defense spending; the prevailing attitude was to spend what was "necessary" for national security. And, under conscription, manpower—the essence of reserve forces—was abundant and relatively cheap.

Pressures to Change the Status Quo

Several recent developments—the federal budget squeeze, a relaxation of East-West tensions, and the end of the draft—have increased the cost of this inertia and should serve as an incentive for decision-makers to scrutinize the reserves more closely.

Fiscal Pressures and Détente

The U.S. defense program is being squeezed between dramatic increases in the cost per unit of manpower and weapon systems, on the one hand, and growing pressures to release defense resources for use in domestic programs, on the other. Large federal deficits in recent years have put decision-makers under considerable pressure from many quarters to reduce military budgets. At the same time, the Berlin agreements, SALT accords, prospects for mutual and balanced force reductions (MBFR) in Europe, and the 1972 presidential visits to Moscow and Peking have seemed to diminish many of the previous fears of a large conventional war in Europe and Asia. Taken together, these developments may bring about a reassessment of conventional force planning assumptions and criteria.

An important signal of U.S. willingness to take a less cautious approach to military planning was evidenced in the retrenchment in 1970 to the one and one-half war strategy put forth in the Nixon doctrine. Despite pressures for not undermining MBFR negotiations, many continue to call for even less conservatism in conventional force planning for NATO, suggesting major changes in NATO planning assumptions regarding length of war and political warning time. Any such reexamination of U.S. conventional forces is bound to have important implications for the mix of active and reserve units.

Table 4-2. Authorized Average Strength of Reserve Forces, Fiscal 1974, and Manpower Shortage or Surplus, by Reserve Component, September 1973

Reserve component	Authorized strength fiscal 1974 (in thousands)	Manpower shortage or surplus, September 1973 (in thousands)	Manpower shortage or surplus as a percentage of authorized strength
Army National Guard	379.1	+5.8	+2
Army Reserve	232.6	−1.1	...
Naval Reserve	119.2	−2.4	−2
Marine Corps Reserve	39.7	−4.4	−11
Air National Guard	92.3	−1.8	−2
Air Force Reserve	49.8	−6.5	−13
Total	912.7	−10.4	−1

Source: Unpublished data from the Department of Defense, Office of the Assistant Secretary for Reserve Affairs, October 1973.

All-Volunteer Reserve Forces[9]

The all-volunteer armed force affects reserve forces in two important ways. First, the end of conscription serves to elevate their responsibility by making them the primary source for augmenting the active forces in an emergency. At the same time, however, it raises a question as to whether enough volunteers can be attracted to the reserves without the costs being prohibitive. Both call for a closer look at the size, structure, and missions of the reserve establishment. Since the Korean war, reserve forces have depended mainly on conscription to fill their ranks. Although no one has been drafted directly into a reserve component, a large proportion of volunteers without prior service have joined under pressure from the draft. In fiscal 1972, an estimated 70 percent of recruits were draft-motivated.

Since draft pressures lessened in 1972, the long lines waiting to enlist in the reserves have dissolved. For example, the numbers waiting to join the Army National Guard shrank from about 100,000 in December 1969 to about 5,000 by December 1971. By September 1973, however, only the Marine Corps and Air Force Reserve components appeared to be having difficulty in maintaining strength; over all, total reserve force shortages amounted to about 1 percent of fiscal 1974 authorized strength. (See Table 4-2.)

These shortages would have been greater had not two programs been instituted in fiscal 1973. First, in conjunction with the need to reduce active

9. This section draws largely on a study made by the Brookings Institution for the Senate Armed Services Committee. See Martin Binkin and John D. Johnston, "All Volunteer Armed Forces: Progress, Problems, and Prospects," report prepared for the Senate Committee on Armed Services, 93 Cong. 1 sess. (1973).

strength, Army personnel were permitted an early discharge if they agreed to serve in an Army reserve component for one year. Second, the policy was established of permitting Selective Service registrants who had already been ordered to report for induction to enlist instead in a reserve unit.

The nature and extent of shortages expected to develop in the future are difficult to estimate. Possible losses and, to a greater degree, recruitment capabilities are very difficult to assess. Reserve components have not kept extensive personnel records, and thus data on expired terms of service, terms of reenlistment, and reenlistment rates have been lacking. Very little is known also about how various incentives affect recruitment for reserve units. Both problems are legacies of the draft. When the draft was in effect, reserve components, having a plentiful supply of "volunteers," did not need to be concerned with such issues. Recent improvements in personnel data processing are expected to provide the means for better manpower planning in the near future.

Table 4-3 shows estimates of reserve gains and losses for fiscal 1974. These data, provided by the services, are based on the assumption that bonuses

Table 4-3. Estimates of Gains and Losses of Reserve Enlisted Manpower, by Service, Fiscal Year 1974

In thousands

Description	Army National Guard	Army Reserve	Naval Reserve	Marine Corps Reserve	Air National Guard	Air Force Reserve	Total
Estimated 1974 beginning strength	344	189	108	39	80	39	799
Expected gains	53	40	25	8	10	11	147
No prior service	31	24	7	4	5	2	74
Prior service	11	9	15	3	4	7	49
Reenlistments	11	7	3	1	1	2	25
Expected losses	65	35	44	11	20	12	187
Difference between expected gains and expected losses	−12	5	−19	−3	−10	−1	−40
Projected 1974 end strength	332	194	89	35	71	39	759
Authorization requested in 1974 budget	346	195	98	37	80	39	796
Projected deficit	14	1	9	2	9	0	37

Source: Department of Defense, Office of the Deputy Assistant Secretary of Defense, Manpower and Reserve Affairs, February 1973. Data reflect latest available service estimates. Figures are rounded.

would not be available for the reserve components. The total expected short-fall below budgeted levels for fiscal 1974 would be 37,000, or about 5 percent of the total. Because of the anticipated inability, without help from the draft, to man reserve units fully, reserve enlisted manpower requested for fiscal 1974 is about 50,000 below "mobilization manning objectives," or the levels at which all units would be completely manned. Against that requirement, the fiscal 1974 shortfall would be close to 90,000, or about 10 percent of the total.

To help close the expected gap, the administration sought authority during calendar year 1973 to use bonuses to attract new volunteers and retain experienced personnel in the selected reserves. The 93d Congress, apparently taking a wait-and-see attitude, failed to take up the proposal in the first session.[10]

Thus, the end of the draft, which has given the reserves a more prominent role in national security, can also be expected to bear heavily on their future size and cost. Both factors make it all the more important to examine the current reserve force structure and to ensure that what the reserves do needs to be done and that they can do it at less cost than equally effective alternatives. These issues are explored in the chapters that follow.

10. Alternatives to using financial incentives to attract volunteers are discussed in Chapter 7.

CHAPTER FIVE

PRUNING NONESSENTIALS

This chapter assesses elements of the reserve forces whose contributions to national security may cost more than they are worth. These include reserve units that appear to bear little relevance to today's needs and units for which equally effective but less costly alternatives exist. The elimination of some of these and the merger of others is considered, along with possible reductions in the size of certain reserve units.

Marginal Functions

Apart from the reserve units comprising the major combat forces discussed in Chapter 2, there is a large number of relatively small, obscure support units and activities whose contribution to national security is difficult to define. Many units, steeped in years of reserve tradition, have been maintained since World War II but now appear to bear little relevance to current needs. Should 7,000 reservists continue to be trained to govern occupied nations? Is there a need for those trained in the administration of art, archives, and monuments to preserve the culture of occupied territories?

Other functions can be questioned on equally valid, if less obvious, grounds. Little is gained by maintaining units whose missions might appear appropriate, but for which personnel with the necessary skills would be readily obtainable from the civilian labor force after mobilization began. The most obvious are medical, legal, construction, and administrative skills.

The total number of reserve billets that could be removed from the reserve structure, on the basis of these criteria, without unduly compromising their ability to support current U.S. military strategy needs detailed analysis. Examination of this question has been avoided in the past because of political and bureaucratic pressures on the one hand, and on the other hand, because of the

Table 5-1. Selected Army and Air Force Reserve Units for Which Reductions Might Be Appropriate

Type of unit	Number of units
Army Reserve	
Adjutant General	155
Army Security Agency	33
Civil Affairs	53
Composite Services (Corps and Field Army Support)	387
Finance	20
Legal	207
Information	92
Medical	389
Military History	12
Military Intelligence	111
Public Information	74
Psychological Operations	30
Quartermaster	33
Signal	144
Training	1,248
Miscellaneous	256
Air Force Reserve	
Medical Service	13
Aerial Port Squadrons	44
Civil Engineering	36
Military Airlift Support	7
Supply	7
Information Security	2
Total	3,353

Source: *Fiscal Year 1974 Authorization for Military Procurement, Research and Development, Construction Authorization for Safeguard ABM, and Active Duty and Selected Reserve Strengths,* Hearings before the Senate Armed Services Committee, 93 Cong. 1 sess. (1973), Part 8, pp. 5750 and 5810.

large number and diversity of the units, which create difficulties in packaging them so as to help decision-makers exert broad policy control.

To illustrate how much manpower might be involved, Table 5-1 gives a partial list of the kinds of units that deserve closer scrutiny. The number of reservists assigned to any one unit is perhaps insignificant in itself, yet the accumulation of these billets—about 150,000—accounts for a substantial share of total selected reserve manpower.

Also deserving attention is the rationale for about 100,000 paid reservists who would be mobilized as individuals—rather than in reserve units—to augment active organizations.[1] This practice, most common in the Naval Reserve, stems from earlier manpower policies under which ships were manned at levels

1. These "individuals," unlike reservists in the Individual Ready Reserve (IRR) category discussed previously, train regularly and are paid.

which, on average, were about 10 percent below full requirements. Under those conditions, the pool of individual reservists was viewed as a source for meeting wartime needs quickly. In the past several years, however, the Navy has been moving in the direction of fully manning its ships in peacetime. In light of these changes, the need for paid individual reservists has become less clear.[2]

The need for some elements of the combat forces is also obscure. The air defense capability currently residing in the reserve forces provides one example. About 4,500 Army National Guardsmen man twenty-seven Nike-Hercules antiaircraft batteries designed to defend against bomber attacks on the United States. Inasmuch as current U.S. policy depends on nuclear retaliatory capability to defend passively against a ballistic missile attack, the logic that calls for actively defending against a less likely and less damaging bomber attack is not persuasive, particularly in view of the annual costs, which exceed $100 million.[3]

Also needing further analysis is the requirement for twenty-one separate combat brigades, including four "special mission" brigades designed to defend Alaska, Puerto Rico, Iceland, and Panama. Active forces routinely deployed in Alaska and Panama should be enough to provide initial defenses; and in the unlikely event that U.S. ground combat forces were needed to defend Iceland or Puerto Rico, other units in the strategic reserve could be used.

Taken together, close to 300,000 reservists (about one-third of the total Selected Reserve) are involved in the functions outlined above; a large proportion appears to be associated with lower-priority activities that can now be considered marginal. It is estimated that at least two-thirds of these billets could probably be reduced without altering essential missions. Savings in pay

2. *Hearings on Research, Development, Test, and Evaluation Program for Fiscal Year 1973 before Subcommittee No. 1 of Committee on Armed Services,* House Armed Services Committee. H. Rept. 92-45, 92 Cong. 2 sess. (1972), Part 3, p. 11694. The growth in ship manning since 1970 provides some evidence of this policy shift; average manpower per ship (not including attack carriers or ballistic missile submarines) has increased by 20 percent between fiscal 1970 and fiscal 1974. Alternatively, the wisdom of abandoning the earlier practice can be questioned. Continuing to rely on reservists to fill out active units in wartime would call for a substantial reduction in active billets. This option is discussed further in Chapter 6.

3. *Fiscal Year 1972 Authorization for Military Procurement, Research and Development, Construction and Real Estate Acquisition for the Safeguard ABM and Reserve Strengths,* Hearings before the Senate Committee on Armed Services (1971), Part 5, p. 3701. Based on average cost per force unit, estimate adjusted by author to include direct support costs. A similar though less compelling argument holds for Air National Guard air defense interceptors. Though questionable for bomber defense, interceptor capability is probably justified for the surveillance of U.S. airspace, for advance warning and to prevent unauthorized overflights.

and allowances alone would amount to about $400 million a year when fully implemented.

Guard-Reserve Merger: Time for Another Try

Both the Army and Air Force have two reserve components, each operating under a different command structure. The National Guard components are administered by the Army or Air Force through the National Guard Bureau, the governors of the respective states, and the states' adjutant generals. The reserve units, on the other hand, are administered by three layers of command. For example, the chain of command for Air Force Reserve units includes Headquarters, Air Force Reserve, one of the three regional headquarters, and appropriate wing/group/squadron elements. Such duplication not only complicates the overall management of the reserve forces but contributes to an unnecessarily large overhead since separate facilities and headquarters staffs are maintained. Moreover, these problems will tend to become more pronounced as recruiting competition intensifies in the absence of the draft.

The merger idea is not new. Following World War II, the "Gray Committee"[4] recognized the disadvantages of the dual organization and recommended that one reserve component be established for each service. Despite the advantages cited by the committee, Secretary of Defense Forrestal did not endorse the recommendation, chiefly because of the "serious schisms which might develop as a result of the kind of struggle which might be precipitated by any effort to secure the requisite legislation."[5]

In 1964 Secretary McNamara resurrected the merger concept for the Army Reserve components. This time, however, in recognition of the powerful constitutional traditions and the local politics associated with the state militia concept, it was proposed that Army Reserve units be combined under the National Guard, leaving intact the forces available to state governors for use in coping with natural disasters and in preserving law and order. After two attempts to push the proposal through the Congress failed, the plan was dropped.

4. This "Committee on Civilian Components" was established by the first secretary of defense, James Forrestal, and chaired by the then-assistant secretary of the army, Gordon Gray.

5. Statement of Secretary of Defense Robert S. McNamara in *Military Procurement Authorizations, Fiscal Year 1966,* Hearings before the Senate Committee on Armed Services and the Subcommittee on Department of Defense of the Committee on Appropriations, 89 Cong. 1 sess. (1965), p. 84.

Secretary Laird showed no interest in taking on this problem. He stated his position on reserve and guard merger before the Senate Armed Services Committee:

We have run into quite a difficult political problem in that the National Guard feels that they have another role to play in their responsibilities to each of our States. I have tackled quite a few problems since I have been over there. . . . I do not think I am going to tackle that one in the next year.[6]

Despite these obvious pressures to maintain separate reserve components, at least two members of the Senate Armed Services Committee appear to favor consolidation. Senator Goldwater, himself a retired general in the Air Force Reserve, has shown particular interest in a merger of Air Force Reserve units, charging that "the State has no use for an Air Guard."[7]

Senator Saxbe, an inactive Army National Guard officer, argues strongly for consolidation:

I am very much alarmed at the failure of the Department of Defense to identify some of the wasted effort. . . . In a county seat town of 10,000 people you have got a Reserve unit and . . . a Guard unit, and they have got a duplication of facilities, and they are fighting over the same man. And this is a waste. I raised this with Secretary Laird and Mr. Kelly. And they said, well, we got a lot of politics involved.[8]

In light of the political realities, one compromise that should be considered is a reorganization that would merge the Army Guard and Reserve into a Guard component and combine the Air Force Guard and Reserve into a Reserve component. The extent of financial savings would depend on how far the consolidation was pushed. The elimination of the Army Reserve command structure and the Air Force National Guard headquarters elements in themselves would yield rather small savings. The further consolidation of guard and reserve base operations, training, and recruiting activities, however, should result in more significant economies. All together, annual savings ranging from $30 million to $50 million could be expected.

Reducing the Size of Reserve Units: The "Cadre" Concept

Raising and training civilian "armies" after mobilization—a practice born out of necessity during World War II—is an alternative to maintaining either active or reserve units during peacetime. The financial implications are obvi-

6. *Fiscal Year 1973 Authorization for Military Procurement,* Hearings, Part 2, p. 551.
7. Ibid., p. 552.
8. Ibid., Part 3, p. 1639.

ous; the costs of a partially manned "cadre unit" would be far less than those of a fully manned one.[9] However, the implications for capability are less clear. Much would depend on how rapidly the cadre, which would have to organize, equip, and train personnel *after* mobilization, could be deployed as a unit relative to how rapidly reserve units that are already organized could be—or would need to be—deployed.

Deployment Time

There is little data upon which to base estimates of the time required to bring cadre units to a deployable status. World War II experience is of limited relevance because the cadres of that day were put together on relatively short notice; and since military equipment was unsophisticated by today's standards, recruits required less technical training than would now be needed. Nevertheless, as is shown below, the average time from activation to deployment for new army divisions during World War II did not vary markedly from the average time between mobilization and deployment for Army Reserve and National Guard divisions.[10]

Category	Number of divisions	Number of months between mobilization/activation and deployment	
		Average	*Shortest*
Active Army	38	24	12
National Guard	18	28	11
Army Reserves	26	22	13

Two considerations would bear heavily on how soon cadre units could be deployed: (1) How soon would new recruits be available?, and (2) once the unit was filled, how much training would be required? Traditionally, new recruits (volunteers or draftees) have been the primary source for forming new units in an emergency. However, with the end of conscription, the selective service, assuming a standby role, will be unable to deliver draftees immediately. Estimates of the delay vary. On the low side, the first draftees should be available about one month after the decision to renew conscription, assuming that the selective service system is maintained to register, process, and give limited numbers of physical examinations. At the other extreme, if the selec-

9. A cadre is a skeleton organization composed of a nucleus of key officer and enlisted personnel who are capable of forming, administering, and training a new unit. Widely used by other nations (Russia, Israel, Switzerland), cadres have not been extensively employed by the United States since World War II.

10. Based on unpublished data provided by the Department of the Army, July 1973. Active Army divisions exclude those activated prior to 1939 and the 2nd Cavalry Division, which was inactivated in North Africa in 1944.

tive service is ultimately dismantled, except for a skeleton staff, it could (based on 1948 experience) take up to six months to deliver the first draftee. These delays could be reduced appreciably if reservists rather than draftees were used to fill up the cadre units. Members of the Individual Ready and Standby Reserves could be expected to report within several weeks following a mobilization order.

The length of the training cycle, including both individual skill and unit training, would also depend on whether those who filled the cadre units were draftees, or reservists with previous military service. In the case of draftees, a full training cycle would be required. Under current peacetime standards, basic and advanced individual training consume about twenty weeks. By tailoring courses to suit the specific needs at hand and exploiting recent advances in education technologies, a well-prepared cadre should be able to bring a division to deployable status, by conservative estimate, within six months. Thus, considering all factors, it would take between seven and twelve months to form, administer, and train a cadre division that had been filled out with draftees.

Where reservists are used to fill the unit, the training cycle can be reduced appreciably. Since a large part of the individual training would be unnecessary, the cycle could be reduced to perhaps four months. Under these conditions, the division should be deployable within twenty weeks after a decision to mobilize. This approach thus is promising for National Guard divisions that, because of readiness problems or existing deployment policies, would not be deployed within that time period.

The deployment capabilities of Army Reserve units are highly contentious. On the one hand, reserve proponents envisage success for Army Reserve units matching that attained by Air Force Reserve units. According to the Deputy Assistant Secretary of Defense for Reserve Affairs, "there is no reason I can see why any type of Guard or Reserve unit which is properly supported and trained cannot match the high state of readiness which has been attained by the Air Reserve Components."[11]

However, basing expectations for the Army Reserve components on the successes achieved by the Air Force Reserve overlooks some important differences between the components. Although the requirement to operate and maintain sophisticated equipment would appear to cause Air Force Reserve units to have more difficulty attaining readiness than would, say, an infantry unit, paradoxically it has been easier for Air Force Reserve units to maintain

11. *Fiscal Year 1973 Authorization for Military Procurement,* Hearings, Part 3, p. 1686.

their proficiency. More Air Force Reserve units are co-located with active units; the logistics, maintenance, and administration support is an obvious advantage. The built-in mobility of Air Force flying units allows them to use distant training facilities; thus more realistic combat training can be carried out on weekend drills. The nature of the Air Force mission permits a greater concentration on individual training and proficiency, as opposed to the larger maneuver exercises necessary to simulate land combat activity. Finally, personnel associated with hardware-oriented units appear to be more highly motivated than those in manpower-intensive land combat units, as evidenced by higher retention rates and fewer disciplinary problems.

Using past mobilization experiences as a guide would appear to call for a good measure of conservatism in estimating deployment capabilities of Army Reserve units. The following table, which summarizes the Korean war mobilization record of national guard divisions, shows that none was deployed within one year of mobilization.[12]

| Division | Date mobilized | Deployed | |
		Location	Date
40th Infantry	September 1950	Korea	December 1951
45th Infantry	September 1950	Korea	January 1952
28th Infantry	September 1950	Europe	November 1951
43rd Infantry	September 1950	Europe	November 1951

The Berlin buildup in 1961 was also met by a partial mobilization of reserves; some 150,000 out of about 2.4 million were activated. Among units called were four Army Guard divisions, forty antisubmarine warfare ships, eighteen naval air squadrons, and ten Air National Guard fighter squadrons. While Air Force and Naval Reserve units were considered operational within several weeks, serious problems for Army components remained in evidence. For some units, it took up to a year of training to become operational; previous planning had assumed that it would take only three to five months. The House Armed Services Committee in 1962, following an investigation of the mobilization problems, concluded that "a significant portion of our present Army Ready Reserve Force is incapable of meeting the increased requirement for readiness now so essential to our national security."[13]

The Vietnam experience cast a stigma on reserve forces that will be difficult to erase. The token mobilizations in 1968 did little to alter the reservist stereotype of that era: impotent, under-equipped organizations manned by affluent,

12. Based on data provided by the Department of the Army, June 1973.
13. Herman Boland, "The Reserves," in *Studies Prepared for the President's Commission on an All-Volunteer Armed Force* (1970), p. IV-2-17.

overqualified, draft-induced "volunteers," who were seeking to avoid almost certain service in Vietnam. Prompted by the Pueblo incident and the Tet offensive, 115 military units consisting of about 37,000 personnel were activated in January and May of 1968. The Army National Guard and Reserve mobilized 76 units, of battalion size or smaller; the Naval Reserve called up 6 fighter aircraft units and 2 mobile construction battalions; and the Air National Guard and Reserve called 5 tactical fighter and reconnaissance groups, 6 tactical airlift groups, and 6 support squadrons. Of the 115 units recalled, 51 remained in the United States, 12 were assigned to Hawaii, 49 were deployed to Vietnam, and 1 each to Japan, Korea, and Europe.[14] These mobilizations got mixed reviews. Several Air Force units that had successfully maintained a high level of readiness deployed within seventy-two hours of mobilization. Other units, which had been only partially manned or equipped, attained "only marginal capability" prior to their mobilization.[15]

This mobilization took place under what should have been "ideal" conditions. Mobilized units were battalion size or smaller; there was adequate planning time prior to call-up; active Army posts were well prepared to receive the units; and the on-going draft was available to supply fillers. Moreover, the number called was small enough so that the best units could be selected. The mobilization, however, was a particular disappointment for some Army Reserve units. A General Accounting Office inspection report pertaining to the mobilization of Army Reserve units concluded that (a) 49 percent of unit personnel were deficient in occupational qualifications, training attendance, and availability, (b) 17 percent were totally unqualified for their assigned positions, and (c) equipment and spare parts shortages were significant.[16] The fact that Army Reserve components were in the midst of a reorganization at that time probably contributed to these deficiencies.

The Cadre Approach

Important implications for the cadre approach stem from this ominous track record. How many combat-ready reserve units could be deployed earlier than could similar units that had been maintained in a cadre status? Of eight national guard combat divisions, for example, how many would be ready for

---

14. Boland, "The Reserves," pp. IV-2-23.
15. Theodore C. Marrs, "National Guard and Reserve Forces," prepared for the Air War College Associate Programs, printed in *Military Capabilities and Employment*, Vol. 3, 7th ed., Maxwell Air Force Base, Alabama: Air University, U.S. Air Force, March 1972, p. 5.
16. Boland, "The Reserves," pp. IV-2-23.

deployment within M+180 days? Though a healthy measure of optimism has been reflected in the publicity accompanying recent administration initiatives to improve the reserves, congressional testimony on U.S. force buildup planning suggests that the Department of Defense continues to take a cautious approach to increasing reliance on reserve forces. Motivated in part by the past performance of reserve units, and possibly by the conviction that current active forces will need but limited assistance to meet the range of likely contingencies, many defense planners appear to be counting on no more than four—and perhaps as few as two—national guard divisions in the first six months following mobilization. According to the previous analysis, those divisions not considered deployable by that time could just as well be maintained as cadre organizations since they could be filled, trained, and deployed as early as could fully-manned units.

The principal critics of this proposal would probably be those short-war enthusiasts interested in maximizing deployments of U.S. combat forces early in a NATO war[17] who hold out hope against historical precedent that, given adequate support, *all* reserve divisions would be made ready in time to influence the outcome. Their concern could be relieved somewhat by limiting the application of the concept to the nondivisional combat battalions, whose missions, for the most part, are less clear than those of the national guard divisions.

Finally, to mitigate the anxiety of those who perceive any compromise of reserve combat capability as posing an unacceptable risk, the approach could be confined to those combat-service support units that together comprise the initial and sustaining support increments discussed previously. These units provide a logical starting point for a test of this concept, inasmuch as cadre support units, which require less training after call-up, could be readied for deployment earlier than could combat units; moreover, many of these units would be needed only in the event that a conflict became protracted.

17. It has been suggested that eighteen U.S. ground combat divisions would be needed in Central Europe within four months after mobilization in order to maintain parity with maximum expected Warsaw Pact capabilities. This deployment schedule could be met with various combinations of active and reserve Army and Marine Corps units. To illustrate, one plausible combination would consist of thirteen active Army divisions (including two redeployed from the Pacific), one active Marine Corps division, and four Army National Guard divisions. Two active and one reserve Marine division would cover Pacific requirements and minor contingencies. In this case, the remaining four national guard divisions would serve as the strategic reserve, principally as a hedge against the possibility that a NATO war would drag on beyond six months. Under these assumptions, a persuasive case could be made for placing these four lowest-priority national guard divisions in a cadre status.

The final determination of the number and type of units that are appropriate for cadre organization needs further analysis. Based on the above discussion, however, it appears that this approach could be applied to a mix of reserve combat and support units roughly equivalent to four divisions without significantly altering current reserve deployment schedules and without sacrificing the effectiveness of the deployed units.

The extent of financial savings from moving in this direction would depend on cadre size. One approach would be to have the cadre consist of all officers and those in the top four enlisted grades at the battalion level, one-half of the officers and top four enlisted grades in the division base, and a modest allowance for skills requiring an exceptionally long training period (for example, tank turret maintenance). For an infantry division composed of eight light infantry battalions and two tank battalions, this option would maintain cadres at about 15 percent of total division strength.[18] Applied to the equivalent of four divisions (with associated initial and sustaining support increments), as was discussed above, this proposal would lead to a reduction of about 150,000 reserve billets at an annual saving—in pay and allowances alone—of about $300 million.

18. Based on data provided by the Department of the Army, July 1973. Assumes G-series Tables of Organization and Equipment for an Army infantry division.

CHAPTER SIX

REPLACING ACTIVE FORCES

This chapter discusses measures for using reserve personnel as substitutes for higher-cost active manpower where this is possible without jeopardizing national security. The proposals lean heavily on a literal interpretation of "total force" policies, advocating an accelerated movement toward a closer integration of active and reserve manpower. Specific examples include: (1) combining active and reserve elements into "hybrid" units; (2) using naval reservists to man vessels undergoing overhaul; and (3) using reserve crews to partially man strategic systems.

Traditionally, U.S. military units in peacetime have been either active or reserve, with the overlap being restricted to a token number of regular military personnel assigned as advisers to reserve units and as staff personnel in reserve headquarters units. Increasingly in recent years, however, the advantages of establishing a closer working relationship between active and reserve units have been recognized. Where these links have been strengthened, improved readiness of reserve units has been evident. The most striking examples are: Army Reserve battalions assigned to U.S.-based active armored divisions; Air Force Reserve crews flying with active units; the integration of Naval Reserve vessels into the active forces; and the large proportion of full-time marines assigned to Marine Corps Reserve units.

Many benefits stem from close active–reserve ties. Full-time administrative, logistical, and maintenance support is made available by the active forces. Reserve units have a greater opportunity to exploit improvements in weapons technology and tactics. Advantages are derived from more direct participation in command and control exercises and from the closer direction provided by professional military commanders. Also, commanders of active units would have more confidence in the reserve personnel under combat conditions than if mobilized reservists were used as fillers, as has been the custom in previous wars. Moreover, a greater sense of participation in a well-defined mission would probably improve the morale of reservists—heretofore considered one of the major obstacles to achieving readiness. This approach would also help to maintain the link between the military and civilian society that many fear will be eroded in the absence of conscription. Finally, improved capabilities for reserve units could make important economies possible through their limited substitution for the more costly active forces. Several examples are discussed below.

"Hybrid" Army Divisions

One promising approach to exploiting the lower peacetime costs of operating reserve units would be to integrate selected reserve elements into Army combat division forces. For example, reserve companies could be assigned to active battalions; reserve battalions could be an integral part of active brigades; or reserve brigades could be combined with active brigades to form hybrid divisions.

Figure 1 illustrates one example of a hybrid Army division integrated at the battalion level. One battalion in each combat brigade would be made up of reservists, as would one-third of each direct-support battalion. Additionally, a proportional share of units in the division base and general support battalion could be reserves. In this illustration, active brigade commanders would be responsible for training, administration, maintenance, and other support of reserve battalions. In the case of division artillery and base, where integration would be at a level lower than that of battalion, the next higher active commanders would be responsible. Active division personnel could monitor and provide assistance for company-level training conducted during normal weekend drill periods, and higher-level training could be scheduled to coincide with active exercises.

At what organizational levels should integration be implemented? How widely can it be carried out? As a rule of thumb, the lower the level at which reserve units are integrated, the less additional postmobilization training is necessary. For a division integrated at the company level, little additional training would be needed since the active command and control structure from battalion through division would be kept intact and ready through routine peacetime training. Much would also depend on the proportions of active and reserve personnel in the hybrid unit. Obviously, the greater the percentage of reservists, the longer the delay in deployment.

For example, by current readiness standards, a division each of whose battalions consisted of one reserve and two active combat-ready companies

Figure 1. Example of a Hybrid Army Division

Shading indicates reserve elements

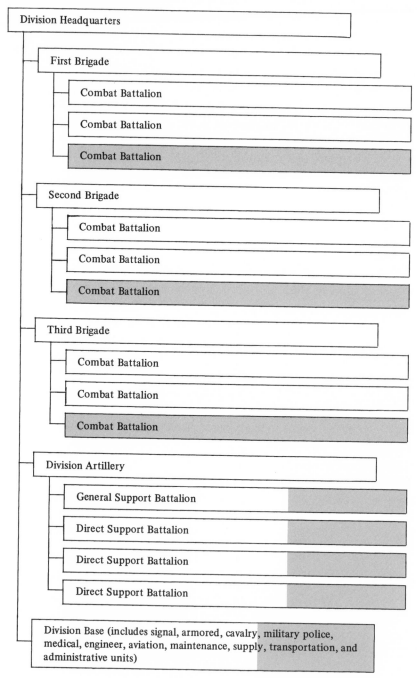

should be deployable within two weeks of mobilization. Where brigades are composed of one reserve battalion and two active battalions, delays of about six weeks could be expected; and where divisions are made up of two active and one reserve brigade, a ten-week delay might be expected.

Apart from the combat divisions discussed above, the concept can be applied, perhaps even more appropriately, to the combat support increments that would deploy with the parent divisions. Being principally support units, they find it easier to maintain peacetime readiness than do combat units; and since most would be deployed as companies or battalions, the need for post-mobilization training would be minimized. For example, command and control exercises required to promote teamwork among rifle companies in an infantry battalion would not be necessary for military police or petroleum supply battalions.

How far could this concept be pushed? Obviously units deployed overseas or those likely to be needed immediately to meet a contingency should not be structured in this manner. For example, U.S. divisions deployed in Europe and Korea should consist of fully active elements. Also units considered to be the primary minor contingency force—such as the 82d Airborne Division—should not be integrated. To do so might put decision-makers in the position of mobilizing reserve units more often than desired, on the one hand, or committing an incomplete contingency force, on the other. The potential implications of integrating active and reserve units can be illustrated by a hypothetical example. As a basis for discussion, a deployment schedule is hypothesized for a NATO contingency (see Table 6-1).[1]

This example will focus on those active divisions judged to be deployable in M+30 to M+60 days. It should be possible to integrate each M+30 division and its associated initial support increment at the company level without affecting its current deployment capability. This option would call for assigning one reserve company-level unit to each active battalion-level unit in the combat division; the resulting division manpower mix would be about 85 percent active and 15 percent reserve. For the associated initial support incre-

---

1. The current U.S. conventional force structure is based principally on meeting the threat of an attack on NATO Europe by Warsaw Pact forces. In a technical sense, U.S. forces for Europe are sized to provide—with NATO allies—enough capability to defend Western Europe successfully. How many forces are needed and how soon they are needed to meet that threat is a highly complex question. The answer depends on assumptions about such factors as the duration and intensity of the war, the amount of political warning time preceding an enemy attack, whether tactical nuclear weapons are used, and whether airlift and sealift are available. Each of these factors is subject to a good deal of uncertainty. Nevertheless, one way to calculate such requirements is based on "force-matching," or examining the manpower and equipment comparisons of friendly and enemy forces under a given set of assumptions.

Table 6-1. Estimated Deployment of U.S. Ground Combat Divisions for a NATO War

Number of divisions

Deployment	Army		Marine Corps		Cumulative
	Active	Reserve	Active	Reserve	
Europe[a]					
M Day	4 1/3				4 1/3
M+15	1 2/3				6
M+30	2				8
M+60	3		1		12
M+90					12
M+120	2	2			16
M+150		2			18
Pacific			1		19
Strategic Reserve		4	1	1	25
Total	13	8	3	1	25

Sources: The deployment schedule shown for current forces is the author's estimate of current U.S. capabilities in light of readiness and airlift constraints, based on analyses contained in Alain C. Enthoven and K. Wayne Smith, *How Much is Enough? Shaping the Defense Program, 1961-1969* (Harper and Row, 1971); John Newhouse and others, *U.S. Troops in Europe: Issues, Costs, and Choices* (Brookings Institution, 1971); Colonel Delbert M. Fowler, "How Many Divisions? A NATO–Warsaw Pact Assessment," *Military Review,* Vol. 52 (1972); and on a Brookings defense analysis study of the U.S. military role in NATO being carried out by Richard D. Lawrence and Jeffrey Record. This deployment schedule assumes that two active Army divisions in the Pacific are redeployed to Europe by M+120 and one active Marine Corps division is deployed to NATO. One active Marine division remains in the Pacific, and two Marine divisions (one active and one reserve) and four National Guard divisions constitute the strategic reserve.

a. "M Day" is the day mobilization of forces begins.

ments, a mix of 75 percent active and 25 percent reserve should not compromise the designed deployment capability.

For the three M+60 day divisions, even larger proportions of reservists could be used. In this case, reserve battalions, or perhaps complete brigades, could be integrated. The scheme that was shown in Figure 1 would result in a hybrid division composed of about 30 percent reserve and 70 percent active manpower.

What risks might be involved in moving in this direction? First, short-war devotees, viewing the importance of deploying ground combat divisions on a more accelerated timetable than the one shown in Table 6-1, might consider the hybrid approach to be too constraining on active force capabilities. By current standards, and based on previous experience, the hybrid divisions discussed above would find it difficult to meet the deployments that would be indicated under short-war assumptions. However, some analysts conclude that hybrid units, if they are designed properly, could be used in these contingencies. If reserve units are located close to the parent active divisions and are overmanned by perhaps 50 percent to assure full manning upon mobilization, it is contended that hybrid divisions with a manpower mix of 86 percent active and 14 percent reserve could be deployed within seven days after mobilization.[2]

Second, those who view the current reserve force structure as vital to national security might argue that the substitution of reserve for active forces would result in a net decrease in total military capability. This concern could be eased by selecting reserve units that, for reasons discussed in Chapter 5, are considered marginal. Army Reserve components consisting of 32 separate brigades and 220 separate battalions provide a pool of units from which to draw. Moreover, implementation of the cadre concept discussed above would provide an additional source of potential reserve manpower.

Taken together, the approach outlined here would substitute a total of about 42,000 Army reservists for active personnel at an annual saving of about $480 million (including a modest allowance for accompanying savings in the active support establishment).

Manning Naval Vessels in Overhaul

Recent moves by the Navy to increase the peacetime manning of naval vessels have important implications for the mix of active and reserve manpower. These policies—ostensibly designed to improve fleet readiness—increase substantially the requirement for active personnel and, as was discussed in Chapter 5, set aside the need for large numbers of naval reservists. This section discusses a measure that would retain a limited number of individual reservists as substitutes for active personnel without compromising fleet readiness.

Naval vessels periodically undergo major overhaul, during which time the ship is out of commission for prolonged periods (from three months for a destroyer to as much as one year for a carrier). While the ship is laid up, full manning authorization is generally maintained. The crew performs routine functions (for example, standing watch and carrying out normal maintenance duties) and assists with overhaul tasks. These functions appear ideally suited for reserve personnel, all the more since the ship would not be steaming during this period. Similar concepts are currently undergoing test. One approach—called "Fourth Watch Section"—begun on fleet destroyers with home ports on the West Coast provides naval reservists to assist in standing watch.[3]

---

2. Based on a Brookings defense analysis study on the U.S. military role in NATO being carried out by Richard D. Lawrence and Jeffrey Record.

3. Admiral Elmo R. Zumwalt, Jr., "Naval Reserve's Role in the Total Force," *The Officer* (July 1972), p. 14.

The extent to which reservists could be used for this purpose needs further study, particularly with respect to geographical considerations. Applying this approach to a carrier task force could result in a direct saving of up to 5,000 active manpower billets.[4] The budgetary savings would amount to about $42 million a year for each task force in overhaul manned in this way.

Of course, much larger savings in active manpower would accompany a reversion to pre-1970 manning policies for all fleet and air units. Pushed to the extreme, this approach could call for active manpower reductions of up to 50,000, with savings of about $400 million a year, but not without some—perhaps significant—sacrifice in capability.

Strategic Offensive Forces

Strategic offensive forces—both aircraft and missiles—have heretofore been the exclusive preserve of the active forces. However, two factors make them appropriate for reserve participation: (1) they are based almost exclusively in the continental United States, and (2) Vietnam experience notwithstanding, their primary mission does not normally require long periods of duty away from their home station.

Strong opposition to the use of reserves in the strategic offensive mission could be expected. First, the high technology associated with strategic systems would be considered by some to require full-time participation to maintain proficiency. On this basis, it would be argued that a reserve bomber crew would be unable to match the effectiveness of a full-time crew. However, reserve crews have attained a measure of success in operating high-performance air defense aircraft. It is assumed, moreover, that the participating reservists would consist principally of prior service personnel, many of whom would have been trained in strategic systems.[5]

Strong concern would also be expected to develop over the wisdom of turning stewardship of strategic nuclear weapons over to part-time citizen-soldiers. This poses a serious question, particularly since the cost of a mistake is so high in strategic warfare. Perhaps the safety procedures used to avoid an inadvertent or irrational action by active personnel could also work with reservists.

4. Based on a carrier task force consisting of an attack aircraft carrier, its air wing, nine escorts, and three underway replenishment ships.

5. The Strategic Air Command has experienced high levels of turnover among crew personnel, thus providing a large pool of potential volunteers. The number that would choose to serve in strategic reserve units, however, is difficult to estimate.

Because of these uncertainties, however, this concept would need to be tested and the results examined closely. Initially, associate crews could be formed to augment existing active bomber and tanker squadrons. As experience is gained, the feasibility of turning complete units over to the reserves should be examined. The current program to disperse strategic aircraft to make them less vulnerable would suit the reserve concept well by providing a broader geographical base for recruiting. The seven squadrons of older B-52s (D models)—the least effective aircraft in the force—and their associated tankers provide a logical starting point. Under current planning, those models will be limited to carrying gravity weapons and are not scheduled to be modified for air-to-surface missile systems (SRAM and SCAD). Moreover, the alert force of about one hundred B-52G-H models maintains substantial nuclear capability.[6] Finally if, as some argue, the principal reason for keeping B-52D aircraft in the strategic force lies in their value as "bargaining chips" for future SALT negotiations, the case for manning them with less expensive reserve manpower is all the more compelling.

Manning the seven B-52D squadrons and an equal number of KC-135 squadrons with a combination of active and reserve personnel similar to the mix currently being applied to Air Force airlift squadrons (about 40 percent reserve) would call for replacing about 1,200 active personnel, which would mean an annual saving of about $16 million.

The intercontinental ballistic missile crews also offer a possibility for combining reserve and active personnel. Because of the remote locations of missile installations and because these units are less manpower-intensive than are bomber and tanker units, the potential for substitution is limited. However, individual reservists or associate operational and maintenance crews could be used to round out active units and alleviate somewhat the manning problems associated with maintaining an around-the-clock vigil over the ballistic missile force.

6. For further elaboration of this issue, see Alton H. Quanbeck and Barry M. Blechman, *Strategic Forces: Issue for the Mid-Seventies* (Brookings Institution, 1973).

CHAPTER SEVEN

COMPENSATION EFFICIENCIES

Two issues related to reserve compensation deserve particularly close scrutiny at this time and underscore the need for a more complete examination of the entire reserve compensation system. The first deals with the use of bonuses to attract volunteers to the reserve components; the second addresses an ineffi-cient feature of the reserve retirement system.

Are Reserve Bonuses Necessary?

As has been discussed above, the administration, envisaging problems in maintaining reserve strength in an all-volunteer environment, has sought legis-lation to establish authority for the secretary of defense to offer bonuses for enlistment and reenlistment. The proposed Uniformed Services Special Pay Act of 1973 would authorize an enlistment bonus of up to $1,100 for a six-year enlistment to an individual with no prior service, a reenlistment bonus of up to $2,200 for someone with a needed skill, and $1,100 for others who reenlist for six years; there are smaller bonuses for those who reenlist for lesser terms. The estimated costs per fiscal year of this proposal are: $85.4 million for 1974, $107.1 million for 1975, $139.7 million for 1976, $97.3 million for 1977, and $108.9 million for 1978.

Until recently, little attention has been given to seeking no-cost or low-cost alternatives to bonus authority. Faced with impending shortages, all the reserves have now stepped up their recruiting efforts. The recruiting funds and manpower for fiscal years 1971-73 and the requests made in the fiscal 1974 budget are as follows:

	1971	1972	1973	1974
Budget (in millions of dollars)	9.1	22.2	40.4	67.5
Manpower (in man-years)	767	1,346	2,434	4,140

Reserve components are also giving increased attention to recruiting more women, nonwhites, and persons scoring in the lower mental groups (as measured by the Armed Forces Qualification Test). Heretofore this large supply of potential volunteers has not been extensively used. Tables 7-1, 7-2, and 7-3 show the proportion each group comprised of reserve accessions in fiscal 1972. The extent to which the reserve components can absorb women and those scoring in lower AFQT Mental Groups is difficult to estimate; proportions for fiscal 1972 active force accessions are shown for comparison. Improved recruiting programs are still in the early stages of development; it would be premature to evaluate them now.

Table 7-1. Recruits Scoring in Mental Category IV[a] as a Percentage of Accessions with No Prior Service, Reserve and Active Forces, Fiscal 1972

Reserve forces		Active forces	
Component	Percent	Service	Percent
Army National Guard	9.5	Army	18.8
Army Reserve	6.0		
Naval Reserve	1.4	Navy	20.2
Marine Corps Reserve	8.3	Marine Corps	22.2
Air National Guard	0.2	Air Force	8.6
Air Force Reserve	6.5		
All components	6.7	All services	17.5

Source: Central All-Volunteer Force Task Force, "Reserve Component Recruiting" (Department of Defense, Office of the Assistant Secretary of Defense for Manpower and Reserve Affairs, November 1972; processed), p. 42.

a. Mental Category IV includes those who score between the 10th and the 30th percentiles on the standardized AFQT test.

Table 7-2. Women Enlisted Personnel as a Percentage of Accessions with No Prior Service, Reserve and Active Forces, Fiscal 1972

Reserve forces		Active forces	
Component	Percent	Service	Percent
Army National Guard	0.004	Army	3.2
Army Reserve	0.2		
Naval Reserve	0.8	Navy	3.5
Marine Corps Reserve	0.2	Marine Corps	1.4
Air National Guard	0.3	Air Force	4.4
Air Force Reserve	0.4		
All components	0.2	All services	3.5

Sources: Reserve components, same as Table 7-1, p. 37. Active forces, Department of Defense, Office of the Assistant Secretary of Defense, Manpower and Reserve Affairs (March 1973).

Table 7-3. Black Enlisted Men as a Percentage of Accessions with No Prior Service, Active and Reserve Forces, Fiscal 1972

Reserve forces		Active forces	
Component	*Percent*	*Service*	*Percent*
Army National Guard	3.7	Army	14.8
Army Reserve	1.5		
Naval Reserve	8.2	Navy	12.5
Marine Corps Reserve	25.3	Marine Corps	17.6
Air National Guard	1.7	Air Force	13.0
Air Force Reserve	2.3		
All components	5.4	All services	14.2

Source: Same as Table 7-1.

Present recruiting practices appear to favor personnel with no prior service. If greater reliance were placed on attracting people with previous service, possible shortages could be alleviated. This would also raise the experience level of the reserves and reduce competition with active forces for recruits. Although information on current programs for recruiting personnel who are leaving active service is sketchy, that which is available suggests that greater counseling efforts and the publicizing of reserve opportunities could yield significant results. The size of this potential source, of course, depends on the number of personnel leaving the service each year. In fiscal 1974, an estimated 360,000 male enlisted personnel will be leaving after their first term. Of these, the reserve components, under current planning, seek to enlist about 49,000, or roughly 1 out of every 7.

On balance, great uncertainty surrounds the whole issue of reserve manpower needs and the success of current recruitment practices in meeting those needs. Moreover, service estimates of expected enlistments are only slightly (5 percent) below fiscal year 1974 authorized strength. With the reasonable probability that this shortfall could be eliminated through some of the measures suggested above, the granting of bonuses could be deferred, pending an examination of the results of these lower-cost programs. This would also encourage further testing of other management initiatives and allow more time for developing a reliable reserve personnel data system. Better estimates of future attrition rates would considerably lessen uncertainty as to recruitment needs. Finally, the reserve manpower reductions that were advocated in Chapter 5 above should, by reducing the magnitude of the recruiting task, lessen the need for new incentives.

Are Reserve Retirees Overcompensated?

Military retired pay is absorbing an increasing share of the defense budget, imposing on the defense program a growing burden that is largely unrelated to current requirements. In fiscal 1973 total military (active and reserve) retired pay of $4.4 billion constituted almost 6 percent of total defense outlays; by 1985 the annual cost will exceed $10 billion, and between now and the year 2000, the cumulative costs will exceed $330 billion.[1] The current military retirement system is a legacy from the period between the two World Wars. At that time the active military establishment was small, and its members served thirty years before retirement. In recent years, however, a combination of much larger standing military forces and more liberal retirement policies (some now retire at age thirty-seven, after twenty years of service) has caused the number of retirees to soar beyond all earlier expectations. Moreover, increases in basic pay (to make military compensation comparable to that in the civilian sector and to provide volunteer service incentives) increased average retirement benefits by about 70 percent between fiscal 1968 and 1973.[2]

Because of the characteristics of the system, not only are changes exceedingly difficult to negotiate, but it takes many years to reap their benefits. In fact, so as not to penalize those already in the system, costs are inevitably incurred in the short run, with savings realized only in the longer term.

The reserve retirement system, still in the incipient stages, will become an increasingly important component of the total military retirement program, reaching a peak in 1985, as may be seen in Table 7-4. Since the major growth in reserve retirement lies ahead, it is sufficiently early to take action to avoid inordinately high costs such as are being experienced in the active military retirement system.

The reserve retirement system is a deferred annuity plan. Retired pay for reservists is computed under the same kind of formula that the active services use; "creditable years of service" determines retirement eligibility.[3] Entitle-

1. This assumes the maintenance of current military manpower levels and annual increases of 5 percent in military basic pay and 1.5 percent in the Consumer Price Index—assumptions used by the President's Interagency Committee on the Study of Uniformed Services Retirement and Survivors Benefits.

2. Basic pay increases varied by grade, ranging from about 70 percent for medium and higher grades and close to 240 percent for recruits. Most retirees are at grades where the increase was about 70 percent.

3. A "creditable year of service" is one in which the retiree earns a minimum of fifty points. Points are earned in a variety of ways: active duty, drills, attendance at schools, correspondence courses, and active membership in a reserve component.

Table 7-4. Annual Disbursement Projections for Military Retirees, 1973-2000ª

Fiscal year	Total annual disbursement (in billions of dollars)	Reserve retiree annual disbursement (in billions of dollars)	Reserve retiree disbursement as percent of total
1973	4.40	0.18	4.1
1975	5.21	0.24	4.6
1980	7.98	0.51	6.4
1985	10.85	0.80	7.4
1990	13.92	0.98	7.0
1995	17.38	1.12	6.4
2000	21.66	1.17	5.4
Cumulative to 2000	339.00	21.70	6.4

Source: Unpublished data provided by the Retirement Studies Directorate, Office of the Assistant Secretary of Defense, Manpower and Reserve Affairs, March 1973.

a. Projections are based on the current retirement system, assuming constant force levels and annual increases of 5 percent in military basic pay and 1.5 percent in the consumer price index.

ment to retired pay vests upon completion of twenty years of creditable service; however, retired pay does not begin until the retiree reaches age sixty. To compute the annuity, "constructed years of service" (total points earned divided by sixty) is used.

One of the most important—and contentious—features is the recomputation privilege, which is unique to reserve enlistment; reserve retired pay is based on the pay rates in effect at the time payments are initiated, rather than those in effect at the time the reservist retires. The implications are far-reaching. For example, a reservist completing twenty years of creditable service in 1968 at age fifty-five would have seen his annuity increase by an average of about 70 percent by the time he started collecting it in 1973. An interagency committee appointed by the President to study the Uniformed Services Retirement System concluded:

A program providing more economic incentive than is necessary to meet its manpower requirements is not efficient. . . . The Committee believes that the present reserve retirement subsystem provides more economic incentive than necessary to meet its manpower requirements by permitting annuity computation to be based on future pay rates, unrelated to the pay level in effect while the member was participating in the reserve service.[4]

The committee recommended that "reserve annuities should be computed on the basis of pay scales in effect at the time the member enters the retired

4. "Report to the President on the Study of Uniformed Services Retirement and Survivor Benefits by the Interagency Committee" (July 1, 1971; processed), Vol. 1, p. 3-2.

reserve . . . CPI-adjusted to time of payment."[5] Eliminating the recomputation provision would produce savings—relatively small at the outset—that would increase to about $300 million a year by 2000. The average annual saving over the period would be about $100 million.[6]

Other Implications

Apart from the two issues discussed here—reserve bonuses and retirement—a more fundamental question in connection with reserve compensation should be noted. Is the same compensation system that was designed primarily to meet the needs of the active forces also appropriate for the reserves? A military compensation system should provide balanced incentives that will attract new personnel, on the one hand, and retain a desired fraction of them, on the other. Basic pay and allowances are critical for the former purpose; retirement benefits become important to the latter.

With the move toward an all-volunteer environment, the compensation system, which had been biased toward rewarding higher-grade career personnel through disproportionately high pay and allowances and retirement benefits, has undergone major changes. In recent years, large increases in basic pay—principally at the lower grades—have reflected concern for the need to attract new volunteers. As this has driven the cost of manpower to record levels, greater attention is now being focused on ways to reduce the retirement element of compensation. These changes can be viewed as shifts to a more efficient compensation mix for the active forces.

There is little reason to believe, however, that this combination of incentives also represents the most appropriate mix for reserve forces. According to the interagency committee,

The Committee believes that an expensive retirement subsystem is not a proper means of motivating high reserve participation levels. If the reserve forces need more members, the appropriate place to direct increased expendi-

5. Ibid., p. 3-7.
6. By way of contrast, federal civilian employees who leave the system short of normal retirement eligibility receive deferred annuities upon reaching eligibility. These annuities, however, are based on salaries that were in effect when the service was performed, *unadjusted* for the Consumer Price Index. Moreover, in recent proposals to reform the military retirement system, the administration has recommended a deferred annuity plan for all active military personnel who leave the system after serving between ten and nineteen years. This annuity, payable at age sixty, would be determined on the basis of the high one-year average of basic pay, adjusted for the CPI to age sixty, but not recomputed as is reserve retirement pay.

tures is into [active] reserve compensation, better equipment, and improved reserve programs.[7]

Very little is known about the priorities affecting the decisions of individuals to enlist or reenlist in the reserve forces; their motivations and needs cannot be assumed to be the same as those of their active counterparts. Perhaps reserve force strength levels can be maintained at less cost than that of the present system. These uncertainties underscore the need for a complete assessment of the reserve compensation system on its own merits.

7. "Report to the President on the Study of Uniformed Services Retirement," p. 3-6.

CHAPTER EIGHT

BROADER CONSIDERATIONS

In exploring possible changes in U.S. reserve forces, the above discussion has centered principally on cost and efficiency factors, under the assumption that alterations in reserve policies geared to these factors could be made without modifying the definition of U.S. interests abroad or affecting present military capabilities designed to protect those interests.

While substantially larger savings could be achieved through greater reductions in reserve forces and greater substitution of reserve for active forces, these would require a reassessment of U.S. commitments—or at least of the military forces needed to fulfill those commitments; both go beyond the scope of this paper. Nevertheless, the sensitivity of the structure of reserve forces to such changes in strategic planning can be illustrated.

One of the most important determinants of the U.S. conventional force posture—both active and reserve—is the assumption made about the expected duration of a war in Europe. Is it reasonable to plan for a conventional war lasting for months or years, or should it be assumed that such a war would end within several weeks on the grounds that either early negotiations or early escalation to nuclear conflict would then take place?

Critics of the current U.S. conventional force posture question both the need for and the desirability of having U.S. forces prepared to fight a long war against a potential adversary that is geared for a short, intense war. According to one source,

Soviet Forces . . . are geared for highly mobile offensive operations aimed at achieving a quick victory. Soviet military strategy, should a major war break out, is to overrun Western Europe before NATO can mobilize and bring to bear its superior manpower and economic resources. This strategy is manifested both in Soviet military doctrine and by the structure of Soviet forces. About three-fourths of Soviet divisional manpower is assigned to combat functions and only one-fourth to support functions. The ratio of tanks (inherently offensive weapons) to men in a Soviet armored division is twice that of

59

a U.S. armored division. Soviet tactical air doctrine emphasizes air defense and close support of ground troops; thus, Soviet aircraft sacrifice range, cost less, and can be procured in greater numbers. In short, Soviet forces are optimized to achieve victory in probably thirty and certainly no more than sixty days. Consequently, their capacity to sustain a longer war would be seriously hampered by distinctly inferior logistic and support capabilities.[1]

If it is correct, this evaluation raises a fundamental question with respect to U.S. conventional forces that has important implications for reserve forces: What purpose is served by maintaining forces that would have little effect on the outcome of a short war in Europe? A decision to design U.S. general purpose forces for a short, intense conflict (assuming—and this is important—that there would be little or no warning time prior to the start of hostilities) would place a premium on forces already deployed or those that could be in place within at most several weeks. Under such circumstances, forces that either could not be deployed quickly or were oriented toward a longer war would have little bearing on the outcome. These would include ground combat forces that could not be made ready for early deployment, naval forces that were committed to keeping Atlantic sea lanes open, and air forces that were oriented toward deep-interdiction missions.

Under the strictest interpretation, the short-war alternative would call for eliminating most Naval and Marine Corps Reserve units, as well as a substantial share of Army Reserve units, with only enough capability being retained to meet domestic emergencies and to provide a modest hedge against the protracted war possibility (perhaps two battalions plus a headquarters in each state). Since many Air Force Reserve units can be deployed rapidly to perform missions appropriate to short, intense wars (such as providing air support and air superiority), the elimination of air reserve units would have to be approached more cautiously. Even if most Air Force Reserve units were maintained, this alternative would reduce U.S. reserve forces to about 350,000 members (about one-third of their current size), which would cost not more than $1.5 billion a year.[2]

Changes of this magnitude, however, that call for major shifts in assumptions underlying current U.S. defense strategy, are not treated in this paper. The following chapter summarizes those recommendations for economies in the use of reserve forces that could be carried out without compromising current military capabilities.

1. Edward R. Fried and others, *Setting National Priorities: The 1974 Budget* (Brookings Institution, 1973), pp. 357-58.

2. This alternative would obviously have a significant impact on active forces as well. For a discussion of these implications and of foreign policy considerations, see ibid., pp. 368-73.

CHAPTER NINE

SUMMING UP

The analysis in this paper is directed principally toward streamlining the reserve forces by phasing out the less effective elements of the reserves and, where appropriate, by assigning to selected reserve units a greater responsibility for meeting current U.S. military commitments. In other words, leaner but more effective reserve forces are advocated. The recommendations, categorized by the branch of the military concerned, are summarized below.

The proposals would impact most heavily on Army Reserve components, which have experienced the greatest difficulties in maintaining readiness and responsiveness. In addition to reducing nonessential or marginally effective activities, three major changes in structure are suggested. First, the headquarters, training, and recruiting facilities of the Army National Guard and Reserve components would be merged. Second, the equivalent of four divisions (including their associated support increments) would be reduced to a cadre status, to be augmented with reservists from the Individual Ready or Standby Reserves upon mobilization. Finally, selected elements of the Army Reserve components would be integrated into five active Army divisions, thus reducing the requirements for active manpower.

In the case of the Naval Reserve, the principal recommendation is a reduction in the present number of individual reservists, for which, in terms of national security, there no longer appears to be a need. Their limited use on vessels undergoing overhaul is proposed, which would permit modest reductions in the use of more costly active manpower.

Proposed changes in Air Force Reserve components center mainly on reductions in lower-priority support forces and reductions that would result from a merger of the Air National Guard and Air Force Reserve headquarters, training, and recruiting facilities. Also advocated is the limited integration of reserve crews into the strategic bomber and tanker forces.

The reductions in reserve strength called for above should make it possible to meet recruitment and reenlistment needs without granting the authority to pay bonuses. Also, it is proposed that reserve retirement benefits be computed on the basis of pay scales in effect when the reservist retires, rather than on the basis of those in effect when the reservist begins to collect his deferred annuity—a feature that is unique to the reserve retirement system. A summary of the manpower and budgetary savings that would result from the proposals made here is shown in Table 9-1. Taken together, these steps would reduce active military manpower by about 60,000 and reserve manpower by about 310,000, and when fully effective would yield average annual savings of about $1.4 billion, at fiscal 1974 prices.

This prescription is intended to provide a reserve force posture that would serve present needs at lower cost. It is based on the view that substantial economies can be achieved in the costs of the reserves without appreciably affecting their present military missions. The efficiencies discussed, while not exhaustive, nevertheless provide a rough measure of the magnitude of the stakes involved.

Beyond this, greater reductions of reserve forces, or greater substitution of reserve for active forces, deserve further exploration. Such an analysis would call for reassessing total U.S. conventional forces, perhaps modifying the definition of U.S. security interests and the military forces needed to protect them.

Changing the shape of reserve forces will not be easy. Though many of the participants in the decision-making process agree that a closer look at the reserves is more important than ever, tough decisions still tend to be avoided because of political and bureaucratic obstacles. The Department of Defense is in the best position to evaluate the structure and size of reserve forces and to initiate orderly programs to redress present imbalances. To encourage it to do so, the following steps should be taken:

First, the National Security Council should direct the Department of Defense to undertake a comprehensive review relating reserve forces to national security policies. At a minimum, this study should explain and justify each reserve unit, activity, and policy and spell out in detail the mission and capability of each unit and the strategy that the unit supports. These data would enable the staffs of the National Security Council and the Office of Management and Budget to identify major reserve force issues, develop alternatives, and establish criteria to help decision-makers choose among these alternatives.

Similarly, the Congress should receive from the Department of Defense an annual report on reserve manpower requirements similar in structure and content to the active manpower requirements report now submitted annually to the Armed Services committees. These reports would permit reserve man-

Table 9-1. Summary of Average Annual Savings from Alternative Reserve
Policies

Policy change	Manpower (thousands)		Dollars[a] (millions)	
	Active forces	Reserve forces	Active forces	Reserve forces
Pruning nonessentials				
Marginal functions[b]	...	200	...	400
National guard/reserve merger[c]	...	10	...	30
Reduce size of certain reserve units[d]	...	150	...	300
Substitution of reserve for active forces				
Hybrid army divisions[e]	50	−42	500	−85
Manning naval vessels[f]	10	−8	100	−15
Strategic forces[g]	2	−1	18	−2
Compensation efficiencies				
Volunteer bonuses[h]	...	...	...	100
Retirement system reform[i]	...	...	...	100
Total savings	62	309	618	828

Source: Author's estimates based on assumptions in notes below.
a. Savings are expressed in constant fiscal year 1974 dollars.
b. Reduction in individual reserve billets (for which incumbents would not be mobilized in reserve units), based on recent changes in defense manpower policies; and inactivation of support units for which a need, in terms of national security, no longer appears to exist or for which there are equally effective and less costly options.
c. Elimination of duplicative national guard and reserve headquarters, training, and recruiting activities.
d. Reducing to a cadre manning level those units that could be expected to be filled out and made ready for deployment as rapidly as could their fully manned counterparts.
e. Integrating reserve battalions and companies into five active Army divisions without noticeably altering current deployment capabilities.
f. Replacing active with reserve manpower on naval vessels undergoing overhaul.
g. Replacing a limited number of active with reserve crews in selected B-52D bomb squadrons and supporting KC-135 tanker units.
h. Assumes that reserve enlistment needs—decreased appreciably by the actions listed above—can be met through measures other than bonuses.
i. Removes the recomputation feature now unique to reserve retirement pay. Savings produced by this change would be relatively small at the outset, growing to about $300 million a year by 2000. The average savings shown would be reached during the 1980s.

power analyses of a greater breadth and depth to be undertaken within the Armed Services committees and would also provide to other interested members of the Congress detailed information with which to make more informed assessments of reserve manpower needs. And, most important, like the National Security Council initiative suggested above, this might encourage a closer examination of reserve issues within the Department of Defense.

Until such steps are taken, it is unlikely that this important element of the defense program will get the attention that it deserves, with the result that spending on reserves may remain higher than necessary to fulfill their existing missions.

DATE DUE

GAYLORD			PRINTED IN U.S.A.